D0538758

West Virginia

WEST VIRGINIA BY ROAD

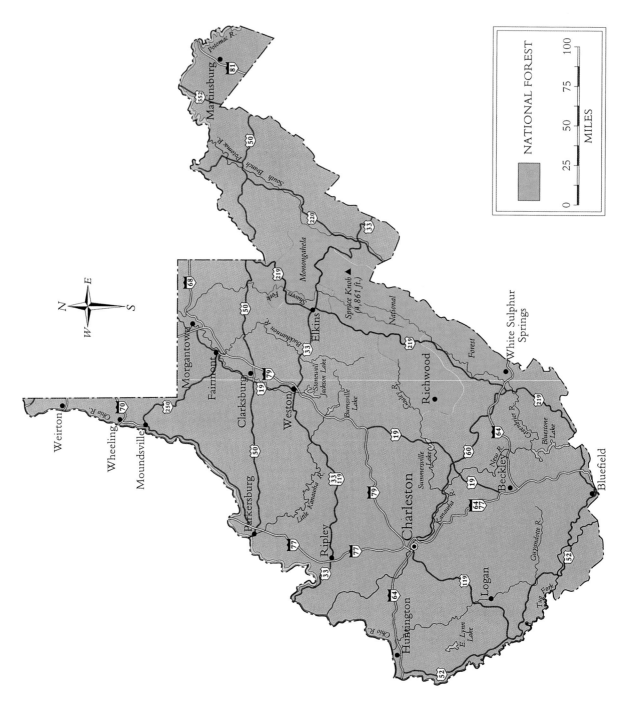

Celebrate the States

West Virginia

Nancy Hoffman and Joyce Hart

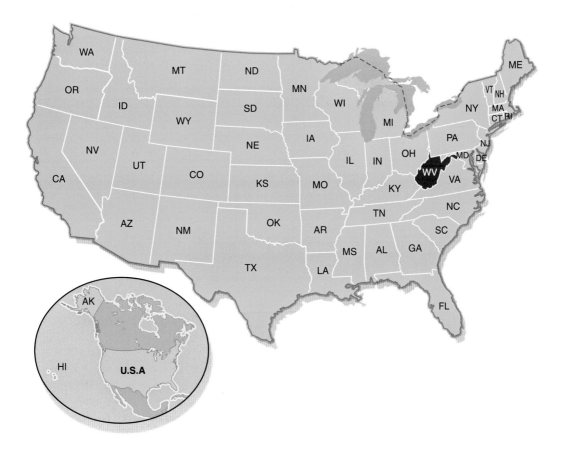

Marshall Cavendish
Benchmark
New York

Marshall Cavendish Corporation
99 White Plains Road
Tarrytown, New York 10591-9001
www.marshallcavendish.us

Library of Congress Cataloging-in-Publication Data
Hoffman, Nancy, 1955–
West Virginia / by Nancy Hoffman and Joyce Hart.—2nd ed.
p. cm. — (Celebrate the states)
Summary: Relates the history and describes the geographic features, places of interest, government,
industry, environmental concerns, and life of the people of this largely rural state.
Includes bibliographical references and index.
ISBN-13: 978-0-7614-2562-5
1. West Virginia—Juvenile literature. I. Hart, Joyce, 1954– II. Title. III. Series.
7241.cbcb.H64 2007
975.4—dc22 2006029393

Editor: Christine Florie
Publisher: Michelle Bisson
Art Director: Anahid Hamparian
Series Designer: Adam Meitlowski

Photo Research by Connie Gardner

Cover Photo: Ron Watts/CORBIS

The photographs in this book are used by permission and courtesy of: *Corbis:* Richard T. Nowitz, back
cover, 54, 68, 85, 89, 90, 92, 95, 131, 135; David Muench, 12, 13, 105; Richard A. Cooke, 15;
Raymond Gehan, 22; Theo Allofs, 23 (top); David A. Northcott, 23 (bottom); CORBIS, 40, 45, 121;
Underwood and Underwood, 44; Kevin Flemming, 56; Stephenson David/Sygma, 64; Ed Eckstein, 78;
H. David Seawell, 81; James L. Amos, 82; Karen Kasmauski, 115; Hulton Deutsch, 119; Wally
McNamee, 127; Kim Kulish, 129; Bettmann, 33, 47, 123. *Dembinsky Photo Associates:* Stephen J.
Shaluta, Jr. , 8; Bill Leaman, 107; Bill Lea, 107 (bottom); Skip Moody, 117. *Getty Images:* Greg Pease,
11; Getty Image News, 17; Jodi Cobb/National Geographic; Skip Brown, 20; Stephen St. John/National
Geographic, 86; Lisa J. Goodman, 87; Pam Francis, 125; Raymond Gehman, 135. *AP Photo:* Bob Bird,
25, 70; Steve Heiber, 74. *Bridgeman Art Library:* Scene near Grafton, West Virginia, 1864 (oil on
canvas), Sontag, William (1822-1900)/Photo c Christie's Images, Private Collection. *The Image Works:*
Topham, 29; Jeff Greenberg, 59, 93. *Art Resource:* Werner Forman, 30. *North Wind Picture Archives:* 31,
35, 39. *Alamy:* North Wind Picture Archives, 38; Jim West, 76, 102; f1 online, 101; Jerry Whaley, 104.
PhotoEdit: Billy Barnes, 63. *The Granger Collection:* 41, 49, 124. *Pat and Chuck Blackley:* 62. *SuperStock:*
James Lemass, 72; Bill Barley, 97; Michael P. Gadomski, 100.

Printed in Malaysia
1 3 5 6 4 2

Contents

West Virginia is mountains.

"The Appalachian hills were aflame in 449 different colors of autumn."
—author Edward Abbey, *The Fool's Progress*

"Mountains run up like walls, with little flat land between, and the people who live there like it that way. They have mortal fear, some of them, of country where there are no hills to protect them from the winds."
—writer Virgil Carrington Jones

West Virginia is wild . . .

"Here are mountain and ripsnorting river and ripsnorting people who came to conquer them both."
—poet Stephen Vincent Benét

. . . and peaceful.

"The very stillness of the place was beautiful. Poverty, serenity and beauty seemed to go hand in hand through the valley."
—longtime Kanawha Valley resident Fanny Zerbe (1928)

West Virginians love to tell stories . . .

"These people were farmers. . . . They brought few books besides the Bible, but in their minds they carried a great store of traditional knowledge and in their hearts a love for the best that had been said in a story and song by their ancestors for countless generations."
—folklorist Patrick W. Gainer

. . . and love their home state . . .

"People leave because they have to, not because they want to."
                    —West Virginia Welcome Center employee Donna Briggs

"But the truth is that most West Virginians of all ages come back continually because they don't feel right anywhere else."
                    —mayor of Richwood, Bob Henry Baber

. . . and are famous for their friendliness.

"In all my travels over the hills and through the hollows for half a century . . . never have I encountered any sign of hostility, but always a genuine show of friendliness."
                    —folklorist Patrick W. Gainer

From the mountains to the valleys below, the natural beauty of West Virginia is apparent from every rock and every bend in the wild rivers. Residents and visitors alike marvel at the breathtaking views.

For many centuries people have enjoyed the bountiful resources that West Virginia offers. However, people who live in this state do face environmental challenges. Rainstorms and snowstorms can quickly turn the beautiful landscape into a nightmare of floods and icy mountain roads. The extraction of natural energy resources can just as well scar the landscape and pollute the water as it can provide West Virginians with income. However, in addition to the challenges is an environment that is not found in any other state—one of flourishing wildlife and natural vegetation, ancient mountain peaks, and a culture of determined individuals who have committed themselves to making West Virginia their home and one of the most scenic states.

Chapter One

Mountainous Wonderland

Over 300 million years ago prehistoric marine life thrived in a sea covering most of what is now West Virginia. Over time the underwater sediment, containing the sunken remains of plant and animal life, hardened to become a thick rock layer. Then two huge masses of this rock, resting on sections of Earth's crust called tectonic plates, began to shift. Their movement was slow—only a few inches a year—but steady. Over the course of fifty million years the movement caused some parts of Earth to crack and crumble and other parts to jut out and up, creating the ridges of what are called the Appalachian Mountains today.

Rich forests and swamps flourished, and the remains of their plant life eventually were buried and slowly became the vast coal, gas, and oil deposits that are still mined in West Virginia. Today, ice and water carve steep ridges and gouge deep ravines where rivers even older than the mountains still flow.

The New River carves its way through the steep mountainsides of West Virginia.

West Virginia is sometimes called the Panhandle State because it is shaped like a large pan with two handles—one in the north and one in the east. Bordered by Ohio in the northwest, Pennsylvania and Maryland in the north, Virginia in the east and south, and Kentucky in the southwest, West Virginia's boundaries are the most irregular of any state.

The only state lying completely within the Appalachian Mountain system, West Virginia has three natural regions: the Appalachian Plateau in the west, the ridge and valley region in the east, and the Blue Ridge region at the tip of the eastern panhandle.

The Appalachian Plateau

In the spring pink, purple, and white rhododendron (the state flower) bloom where sunlight falls in the dense forests of the Appalachian Plateau. Deep river valleys rise and fall across this region, eventually intersecting with the rugged Allegheny Mountains, which divide the plateau from the eastern part of West Virginia. The Appalachian Plateau challenged early settlers and pioneers attempting to cross it. Altina Waller wrote, "Towering mountains obliterated the sun for many hours a day and impeded travel except along creek beds and rivers." Flat land is rare in this region, but what there is of it is usually populated, even though the flatlands are often prone to flooding.

The Appalachian Plateau contains large deposits of coal, oil, gas, salt, and iron ore. The Kanawha Valley breaks up the rural landscape with miles of chemical plants, which border the Kanawha River and surround Charleston, the state capital. Along the valley the fresh mountain air has been replaced with the smell of industry, and the valley grasses have been covered with cement pavement and asphalt roads.

The Allegheny Mountains extend from Pennsylvania through Virginia, crossing the back country of West Virginia.

The Ridge and Valley Region

From the barren, rocky tops of West Virginia's highest peaks, climbers can see how vast and beautiful this region is. The towering mountains roll down to fertile green valleys. This is the ridge and valley region.

Eagles and hawks circle the sky and land on windswept trees. Bogs more commonly found in arctic tundra have found their way into this region in such places as Dolly Sods and Cranberry Glades. Mountain laurel, which looks like a delicate version of the rhododendron, grows in abundance just below the rocky peaks, as do huckleberries, which look and taste like blueberries.

Azaleas bloom in Dolly Sods National Wilderness and Scenic Area.

CRANBERRY GLADES

One of the strangest parts of southwestern West Virginia is Cranberry Glades, a piece of arctic tundra pushed into Pocahontas County by glaciers millions of years ago. Tundra is a treeless, sometimes boggy plain found in cold, northern climates. Even though the glaciers retreated from West Virginia long ago, visitors always take along a jacket when visiting the glades, because the weather often shifts from warm to cold in an instant.

Cranberry Glades is a 750-acre bog with spongy ground made up of partially decayed plants, called peat. Visitors must stay on a boardwalk to avoid being ankle-deep in water. This is an especially good idea because of the large-leafed skunk cabbage, which smells like its namesake.

Cranberry and insect-eating plants creep along the floor of the bog. The cranberry plants are well camouflaged by their reddish green color. The most unusual part of the glades are the amazing insect-eating plants. These plants do not have teeth. Instead, they trap bugs and then digest them with juices they secrete.

LAND AND WATER

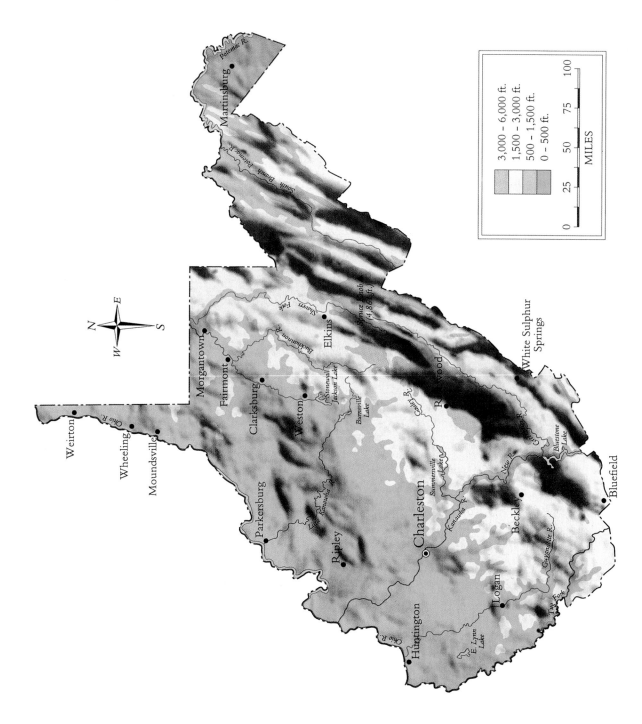

Martinsburg

Potomac R.

South Branch Potomac R.

Spruce Knob
(4,861 ft.)

White Sulphur
Springs

Morgantown

Fairmont

Shavers Fork

Buckhannon R.

Elkins

Clarksburg

Weston

Stonewall
Jackson Lake

Burnsville
Lake

Greenwood

Gauley R.

Weirton

Ohio R.

Wheeling

Moundsville

Parkersburg

Little Kanawha R.

Kanawha R.

Summersville
Lake

New R.

Greenbrier R.

Bluestone
Lake

Bluefield

Beckley

Charleston

Ripley

Kanawha R.

Logan

Guyandotte R.

Tug Fork

Ohio R.

Huntington

E. Lynn
Lake

3,000 – 6,000 ft.
1,500 – 3,000 ft.
500 – 1,500 ft.
0 – 500 ft.

MILES

0   25   50   75   100

This region includes the Allegheny Mountains, which rise along the eastern border and include most of the eastern panhandle. Ridges are covered with trees and rise to between 3,000 and 4,000 feet. The valleys have rich soil, which farmers use to grow crops. This area is an awe-inspiring countryside, full of spectacular vistas and lovely meadows. The majestic beauty inspired the well-traveled author Pearl S. Buck to proclaim her native West Virginia to be the "world's most beautiful place."

The Blue Ridge Region

"The passage of the Potomac through the Blue Ridge," wrote Thomas Jefferson, "is perhaps one of the most stupendous scenes in nature." Watching the Potomac River flow between the mountain ridges, Jefferson wrote that he had the feeling that, long ago, waters had been dammed up in the hills until at last they "broke over at this spot and tore the mountain down from its summit to its base." The narrow strip of land to which he was referring is Harpers Ferry, the state's lowest point, at 247 feet above sea level.

Harpers Ferry is located at the meeting place of the Potomac and Shenandoah rivers.

The Blue Ridge region includes the stunning Shenandoah Valley, which is full of apple and peach orchards. Even as he was being led to his execution in this area, the abolitionist John Brown said to the jailer accompanying him, "This is beautiful country. I never noticed it before."

FAST-FLOWING RIVERS

When the explorers Thomas Batts and Robert Fallam crossed the Appalachian Mountains in 1671 and came upon the New River, they were astonished to find it flowing west. The New River is a mysterious, unpredictable, and ancient river even older than the Appalachian Mountains. Northeast of the New River, rivers flow into the Atlantic Ocean. Southwest of the New River, most rivers flow into the Ohio River. When the ancient mountains were thrust up, the New River cut its own route, creating spectacular canyons and gorges along the way. Some authorities say that at one time, even the mighty Mississippi River was a tributary of the New River. This river has changed course and direction since ancient times. Now the New River flows quietly into the Kanawha River, and together these two rivers cut across the entire state.

Much of the New River is not safe to swim in. Whirlpools pull unsuspecting swimmers below the water's surface. The river also has a dangerous undertow. But because it is so wild, the New River has become an important part of the state's growing white-water-rafting industry. Many people visit West Virginia to ride the state's rapid rivers. Even though the New River is considered a wild river, it is the dam-released Gauley River that is often referred to as the ultimate white-water challenge, because the ride is so exciting. The Gauley River has been described as "a roller coaster of rapids with no calm spots in between."

White-water rafters brave the fierce waters of the New River.

Not all of West Virginia's rivers are quite as fierce as the New and Gauley rivers. In the north the Cheat, Tygart, and the south branch of the Potomac River are all good rivers for rafting and canoeing in the spring. The Shenandoah River in the eastern panhandle and the Greenbrier River in the south are great for first-time paddlers looking for scenic beauty, historic sights, and a somewhat calm float down a West Virginia river.

West Virginia's variations in altitude cause variations in climate. Thick fog and several feet of snow often cover the mountain peaks. Winter cold and snow hit higher elevations even harder. In Elkins, a town with one of the highest elevations in the state, January temperatures can range between 22 and 43 degrees Fahrenheit. But the coldest temperature ever recorded in West Virginia occurred on December 30, 1917, with −37 °F recorded in Lewisburg.

The state capital, Charleston, is located in the Kanawha River valley. During the summer Charleston is considerably warmer and more humid than the surrounding mountain areas. Many people who work in Charleston live in nearby mountain towns and look forward to going home and escaping the valley's heat and humidity.

Fog hangs over West Virginia's Tygart Valley.

Bluefield, West Virginia's highest city, sitting at 2,655 feet, is a mountain town in the state's southernmost community. Bluefield calls itself "nature's air-conditioned city." To emphasize how cool the summers are in town, Bluefield's merchants have promised to serve free lemonade whenever the mercury hits 90 ℉, which has happened only a few times. One of those times was during a massive heat wave in the summer of 2006. Krysta Lawrence, a Bluefield State College student, helped hand out free lemonade. "I think it's important to give something back to your community," Lawrence said. "This has been a lot of fun."

FREQUENT FLOODING

The average annual rainfall in West Virginia is only about 42 inches per year. However, the annual rain received varies greatly from area to area. For instance, West Virginians living in the mountains might see as much as 100 inches of precipitation in one season, while people living in the shadow of the mountains (on the dry side) might only experience 30 inches.

Rainfall in West Virginia is produced by three main weather conditions. In the summer thunderstorms are quite common and can cause sudden downpours. In the fall remnants of hurricanes blowing north from the Gulf of Mexico can dump a lot of rain on the state. And in the winter stalled storm fronts that have arrived in the state from the Atlantic Ocean often produce a lot of rain or snow. All three types of storms have the capability of producing enough precipitation to cause massive flooding.

Some years in West Virginia are worse than others, but every year the state experiences damaging floods. For example, in 2005 President George W. Bush declared six counties in the northeastern part of the state as disaster areas due to heavy rains and flooding. In 2003 and 2004 seven counties in the northwestern section of West Virginia were damaged by floods.

Residents navigate downtown Harpers Ferry after heavy rains caused flooding.

Between 2001 and 2004 West Virginia suffered from more floods than ever recorded. The total damage was estimated to be $1.5 billion. The combination of heavy precipitation and the many deep and narrow valleys in the state create the perfect conditions for massive flooding. However, many people in the state are starting to point their fingers at mining and logging companies for making the flooding worse. Many environmentalists and scientists believe that strip mining and deforestation increase the possibilities of flooding. However, since many West Virginians depend on the mining and forest industries to make a living, the fight to lessen the annual flooding damages may take a long time to win.

PLANT AND ANIMAL LIFE

Hundreds of years ago West Virginia was covered by magnificent forests. Fires, logging, mineral extraction industries, and pioneering farmers wiped out those once-towering woods. Today, second-growth and later-growth trees cover about four-fifths of the state. Evergreen forests of white pine, red spruce, and hemlock cover mountain slopes and border riverbanks.

Cathedral State Park is a majestic stand of virgin hemlock and hardwood trees. These ancient trees are just as they were before humans invaded these mountains. A walk through the grove is a little like going back in time. A floor of dark green moss and an abundance of ferns add to the mysterious atmosphere of this park.

Flowers of all kinds can be found in the state. Wildflowers border even newly built highways. Red poppy, purple clover, white daisy, and yellow black-eyed Susan make a drive up Interstate 79 pleasant.

Hundreds of years ago, bison, elk, bear, cougar, deer, and other large mammals roamed the state's rugged terrain. After seeing the

Kanawha Valley in 1770, George Washington wrote, "This country abounds in Buffalo [bison] and wild game of all kinds, as also in all kinds of wild fowl, there being in the bottom a great many small grassy ponds or lakes which are full of swan, geese and ducks."

What Washington saw has changed. Strip mining, mountaintop removal, and pollution from the chemical industry have killed off much of West Virginia's game and fowl. Most large species have disappeared. However, deer are still numerous, and black bear have increased their numbers in recent years.

A large herd of white-tailed deer graze on a West Virginia farm.

The fox makes its home in the forests of West Virginia.

New conservation methods are beginning to bring back some of what Washington found so plentiful. Restored strip-mined and deforested land has ensured the survival of many small animals, including beaver, otter, marten, mink, bobcat, fox, and groundhog. Similar efforts have brought back fish once endangered by wastes from mines and sawmills. Mountain rivers and streams are again full of trout, walleye, bass, and pike due to the efforts of conservationists to keep the state's rivers and creeks stocked.

West Virginia is alive with songbirds, including cardinal (the state bird), wood thrush, brown thrasher, and scarlet tanager. Hawk, eagle, and falcon live on mountain peaks. Quail, woodcock, and snipe join such migratory birds as loon, duck, geese, and grebe on small lakes and ponds.

There are lots of snakes in West Virginia—twenty species in all. Two types are poisonous, the timber rattlesnake and the northern copperhead. Hikers are most likely to see copperheads in the southern West Virginia state parks of Little Beaver, Grandview, and Babcock. It is also not unusual to see rattlesnakes in the northern parks of Canaan Valley and Blackwater Falls.

The northern copperhead is usually seen in southern West Virginia.

West Virginia is rich in deposits of coal. However, recent developments in the method of removal of coal from the state's mountains are causing widespread controversy. A rapidly growing number of mountains in the Appalachians are literally losing their tops to mountaintop removal (MTR).

MTR is the process in which 800 feet or more of rock is blasted off the tops of mountains in order to allow mines to more easily reach veins of coal. The resulting rubble (rocks, trees, and other debris) is then pushed down the mountainside into the valleys and rivers below. According to the U.S. Environmental Protection Agency, the practice of MTR in the past two decades has caused damage to the environment. Some of this damage in West Virginia includes the burial of rivers and streams and the loss or pollution of drinking-water sources. Complete villages have also been wiped out, forcing people to leave mountains on which their families have lived for hundreds of years. Wildlife is also affected by the loss of habitat and the pollution of water. As the state loses some of its natural beauty, tourists become less interested in visiting, causing a loss of revenue.

On the other side of the issue is the constantly increasing need for energy resources in the United States. Coal is considered a valuable commodity in the effort to produce clean energy. MTR mining produced 40 million of about 150 million tons of coal produced in the state in 2004. Coal mining also creates about 40,000 jobs for West Virginians, about 18 to 19 percent of the state's jobs. In addition, coal-mining companies pay about $70 million each year in state taxes, fueling the state's economy.

After a mining company removes the top of a mountain and completes the mining process, according to law, that company is supposed to restore the mountain as much as possible to its original state.

Mountaintop-removal mining has flattened many mountain peaks in West Virginia.

The company is then responsible for turning the land into a usable plot for the citizens of the state. This has not always happened.

However, the mining industry claims that improvements are being made. To demonstrate this, several mining companies have won state and federal awards for their efforts in restoring old coal mines.

Chapter Two

Appalachian Frontier

People first inhabited the Kanawha Valley more than 12,000 years ago. These people, the Paleo-Indians, used sharp stone tools and spearheads called Clovis points to slay large mammals, such as mammoth, mastodon, and caribou. Archaeologists have found these tools in the mountains and along river bottoms as well as on Blennerhassett Island and in Peck's Run, in Upshur County. Many ancient arrowheads have also been found along the Ohio River between Saint Marys and Parkersburg. Paleo-Indians also hunted smaller animals and gathered plants. Paleo-Indians were nomadic people, meaning they moved a lot, following the migrating herd of animals and the changing seasons. Scientist's knowledge of the Paleo-Indians is filled with big gaps. No one knows for sure what happened to these early people. They may have moved on to other places. They may have all died. Or, as some people believe, they may be the ancestors of new tribes of Native Americans who appeared later in what is now West Virginia.

ARCHAIC PEOPLE

Around 7000 and 1000 B.C.E. new tribes of people arrived in what is now known as West Virginia. Archaeologists have discovered the remains of

William Sonntag painted this scene of rural West Virginia in 1864.

villages in the northern panhandle, the eastern panhandle, and the Kanawha Valley. These people, sometimes referred to as the Archaic people, are believed to be the ancestors of some modern Native Americans. The Archaic people were not nomadic like the Paleo-Indians. They built villages and created gardens. Those who lived near rivers caught fish to supplement their diets. There is an ancient site in Saint Albans in Kanawha County that is believed to be the first permanent settlement in what has become the state of West Virginia.

ADENA CULTURE

The Adena people lived in the area that is now West Virginia between 1000 B.C.E. and 500 B.C.E. The Adena were even more rooted to the ground than the Archaic people. Village life was more organized, and there are records indicating that the Adena even had time, above and beyond ensuring their survival, to organize sporting games. The Adena are also one of the first groups known to have buried their dead in burial mounds. Two of the more significant of these mounds are the Grave Creek Mound in Moundsville and the Criel Mound in South Charleston.

The Adena were also hunters and gatherers. Women and children gathered nuts, roots, berries, seeds, and leaves, while the men went after game. Their clothing was probably made of deer hide. Tools were made from stone, bone, wood, and deer antlers. Arrowheads, knives, scrapers, and drills were made from flint—a hard stone found along the banks of the Kanawha River. Pottery was made by digging up clay from the riverbank and mixing it with crushed mussel shells.

By about 1500 C.E. the Mound Builders had abandoned their villages. No one knows exactly what happened, but experts think that warfare, disease, or lack of rain may have forced them to leave their homes.

Grave Creek Mound is one of the largest burial mounds in West Virginia, requiring more than 60,000 tons of earth.

HOPEWELL CULTURE

What scientists refer to as the Hopewell Culture existed in the area that is now West Virginia between 1 C.E. and 1000 C.E. Hopewell were also Mound Builders, and they also built mile-long stone walls, such as those found at Mount Carbon. Some people believe these walls may have been built around villages. Others think that the stone walls might have protected what the ancient people designated as sacred ground. Many of these walls have been destroyed over the years, some by the practice of mountaintop-removal mining.

A figurine of a Hopewell woman dates back to 300 B.C.E.–500 A.C.E.

In the years between the appearance of the ancient Mound Builders and the appearance of European explorers and settlers in the area of West Virginia, many Native-American groups either traveled through the land or built settlements. Others hunted the abundant wildlife in the mountains and along the rivers and streams, but lived in other areas. Still other Native peoples moved to the area to get away from warring tribes. Some of the cultural groups that might have lived in or around this area included Shawnee, Cherokee, Delaware, Seneca, Wyandot, Ottawa, Tuscarora, Susquehannock, Huron, Sioux, Mingo, and Iroquois.

Native Americans gather maize and squash.

By the 1640s this region was primarily a hunting ground for members and allies of the powerful Iroquois Confederacy, a group of eastern Native-American people that banded together. Some historians have suggested that members of the Iroquois Confederacy used their joint power to force all other cultural groups to leave the area, protecting what is now West Virginia as the confederacy's private hunting grounds.

When the first European settlers arrived in what is present-day West Virginia in about 1730, only a few Tuscarora, Mingo, Shawnee, and Delaware, who were all connected with the Iroquois Confederacy, lived in the area.

EUROPEAN EXPLORERS

John Lederer, a German physician, is credited with being the first European to see West Virginia. Commissioned by Virginia's royal governor, Sir William Berkeley, Lederer made two trips to the top of the Blue Ridge in 1669 and 1670. Lederer appears to have been very dramatic and a bit of an exaggerator. He recorded accounts in his travel journals of giant snakes, ravenous wolves, lions, peacocks, and mountains so high he could see "the Atlantick-Ocean washing the Virginia Shore."

In 1671 the Englishmen Thomas Batts and Robert Fallam crossed the Appalachians and found a river that flowed into the Ohio River. It was probably the New River, or possibly the Tug Fork. This discovery led England to claim the Ohio Valley as its own.

Perhaps the most famous early traveler to western Virginia was George Washington. In the late 1740s, at age sixteen, Washington joined a party of surveyors working for Baron Thomas Fairfax, a wealthy Virginia landowner. They crossed the Allegheny Mountains into what is now West Virginia. At that time Appalachia was the frontier of North America.

The young George Washington first visited West Virginia as a land surveyor.

The people who lived there were accustomed to living without the comforts that many people living on the East Coast took for granted. According to Washington, one night he "went in to ye Bed as they called it when to my Surprise I found it to be nothing [but] a Little Straw matted together without sheets or anything else [but] only one thread[bare] blanket with double its weight of Vermin such as Lice, Fleas." As he got older, Washington grew to love the frontier and learned to respect the hardiness of its settlers.

In 1754 the struggle between the British and the French over territory in North America erupted into open conflict in the French and Indian War. Virginia's colonial governor promised land to men who enlisted to defend the frontier. George Washington fought as a commander for the British.

After the British won the war, Washington was visited almost daily by men who had served under him and who looked to him to help them claim their land. This was no easy task, because the British government, the Virginia Assembly, and various land companies opposed keeping the promises they had made to the militia veterans.

Washington left for the Ohio Valley in October 1770 to help the former soldiers and to obtain land for himself. He succeeded in doing both. Washington planned to return to the frontier in 1773 to begin surveying his land, but he never did.

CONFLICTS WITH SETTLERS

After the French and Indian War ended, thousands of pioneers made their way to Virginia's western frontier. Many built homes in the Ohio River valley on land that Native-American nations had not given up. As a result settlers and Native Americans often clashed violently. According to one missionary named John G. Heckewelder, white frontiersmen often claimed that killing Native Americans was the same as killing bears. Despite the conflicts, one Mingo chief named Tah-gah-jute had been particularly friendly with white settlers. He was even baptized a Christian, at which time he took the English name James Logan, in honor of William Penn's (the governor of Pennsylvania) secretary, a friend of the Native-American people. Logan enjoyed living close to the white settlers, but his sentiments soon changed drastically. In 1773 a group of white men went on a murderous spree against the Shawnee and other Native Americans. On April 30, 1774, some of these men massacred and scalped a dozen peaceful Mingo. Among those killed were Logan's father, brother, and sister, who was pregnant.

Logan was angry. Seeking revenge, he went on a rampage, killing at least thirteen settlers that summer. Later in the fall Logan joined forces with the

Many pioneers settled in West Virginia, often on Native-American land. This illustration shows a log cabin at the base of the Seneca Rocks.

Shawnee chief Cornstalk to fight the forces of Lord Dunmore, the governor of the Virginia Colony. Contrary to a proclamation passed in 1763 that prohibited European settlements west of the Appalachians, Lord Dunmore sent an army into Shawnee territory to help settlers take land from the Native Americans. That conflict, known as Lord Dunmore's War, occurred on October 10, 1774, and ended with the defeat of the Native-American people living near the Ohio River at Point Pleasant.

Chief Cornstalk agreed to a peace treaty with Dunmore's armies, but at the treaty's signing, the chief spoke of the Virginians' sins and broken promises and openly accused them of inciting the war. As a result of losing the battle, the Native Americans were forced to give up their land.

CHIEF LOGAN'S LETTER

James Logan did not attend the peace negotiations at Point Pleasant. Instead, he sent a letter expressing his outrage over the actions of the white settlers:

I appeal to any white man to say if ever he entered Logan's cabin hungry and he gave him not meat, if ever he come cold and naked and he clothed him not?

During the course of the last long and bloody war, Logan remained idle in his camp, an advocate for peace. Such was my love for the whites that my countrymen pointed at me as I passed and said "Logan is the friend of the white man." I had even thought to have lived with you but for the injuries of one man. Colonel Cresap, the last spring, in cold blood and unprovoked, murdered all the relations of Logan, not even sparing my women and children. There runs not a drop of my blood in veins of any living creatures. This called on me for revenge. I have killed many. I have fully glutted my vengeance. For my country I rejoice at the beams of the peace; but do not harbor a thought that mine is the joy of fear. Logan never felt fear. He will not turn on his heel to save his life.

Who is there to mourn for Logan? Not one.

In 1775 the American Revolution broke out. Most of the Native peoples in what is now Ohio sided with the British, who armed them to fight the rebelling colonists. Still, peace reigned in western Virginia until the spring of 1777—a time often referred to as the bloody year of the three sevens. Americans were settling on land protected by treaties made between the British and Native Americans. Because the British did not want rebelling colonists to take over the frontier, they encouraged the Native Americans to defend their hunting grounds with force.

Chief Cornstalk warned all sides that blood would flow as never before. He admitted he was powerless to stop it, but still he tried to bring peace. Accompanied by a young Shawnee chief named Red Hawk, the old leader went again to Point Pleasant—this time to warn Captain Matthew Arbuckle about the growing tension between the Shawnee and the white settlers. But the two chiefs were taken prisoner and held as hostages. Chief Cornstalk knew that he would likely be killed. He said, "When I was young and went to war, I often thought each would be my last adventure and I should return no more. I still live. Now I am in the midst of you and if you choose, you may kill me. I can die but once. It is alike for me whether it is now or hereafter."

Several days later a white soldier was killed and scalped outside the fort. With a cry of "Let us kill the red dog," a group of soldiers took over the fort. They wanted to kill the captured chiefs and Cornstalk's son, who was visiting him. The soldiers threatened Captain Arbuckle with death if he tried to stop them. Cornstalk was warned of the mutiny, but made no attempt to escape. Instead, with great dignity he walked toward the murderous men. He took seven bullets in his body before falling to the ground without even a groan. The other two Native Americans were also slain.

The British encouraged the Native Americans to fight against the settlers during the Revolutionary War. For instance, in 1778 British soldiers worked with Mingo men to launch an attack on several forts. One of the bloodiest battles of the Revolutionary War in the area that is now West Virginia occurred at Fort Henry, near present-day Wheeling. The battle began on September 10, 1782, and lasted three days. The colonists proved too strong for the British

During the Revolutionary War Native-American tribes fought alongside British soldiers to protect and to keep their land.

and Native-American forces and withdrew. Shortly afterward, the British ceased their attacks in the frontier land. After the Revolutionary War ended in 1783, most of the Native-American population moved farther west. This did not end the conflicts between the Native people and the new settlers in what would become West Virginia, however. That would not happen until 1794, when General Anthony Wayne defeated a band of Native Americans at Fallen Timbers in what would later become the state of Ohio. Due to this defeat the Native-American tribes were forced to sign the Treaty of Greenville in 1795, which took away all Native-American claims to land in what would become West Virginia.

After the Revolutionary War western Virginia was still considered the frontier. It attracted such adventurers as Daniel Boone, who came to the Kanawha Valley in 1788, after losing his holdings in Kentucky. Boone always looked like a frontiersman, carrying a tomahawk and his favorite bear trap, "Old Isaac." Traveling far and near, he hunted beaver, otter, fox, and raccoon.

In 1791 he settled near what would become Charleston. He was elected to represent Kanawha County in the state government. The 1790s were a time of peace and transition in western Virginia. Boone resisted the changes. He became restless, longing for new lands to explore and conquer. In 1795 he left the Kanawha Valley for Missouri.

Industry was developing in the mountains of western Virginia. In 1794 an iron furnace was built at King's Creek. The first salt well was drilled in the Kanawha Valley in 1797. By 1808 salt production had increased from 150 to 1,250 pounds a day. At about the same time oil and natural gas were discovered in the region, and the first steamboat began operating on the Ohio River, opening up water transportation in the area.

The people in the western region became increasingly unhappy with their parent state. For the most part people in western Virginia were not slaveholders. Many openly opposed slavery. They also felt their political representation was too small in Virginia's government.

During the late 1700s West Virginia produced more than 1,000 pounds of salt per day.

As early as 1810 western Virginians had officially protested that they were not getting equal representation in the Virginia legislature.

In 1859 something happened in the town of Harpers Ferry. There, the Potomac and Shenandoah rivers meet. And there a spark helped ignite a war, dividing a state and a nation.

JOHN BROWN'S RAID

The abolitionist minister Henry Ward Beecher called him a "crazed old man." The African-American leader Frederick Douglass found him eloquent. The Confederate general Thomas "Stonewall" Jackson thought him a brave but misguided man. And the French writer Victor Hugo said, "he was an apostle and a hero. [His death] has only increased his glory, and made him a martyr."

John Brown referred to himself as a "determined abolitionist" who swore "eternal war with slavery." His description rings true. Even before that day in Harpers Ferry, he led raids into Kansas in which proslavery advocates were captured and killed.

Brown went to Harpers Ferry hoping to start a slave rebellion in Virginia. On Sunday, October 16, 1859, Brown, five black men, and sixteen white men prepared to raid the federal arsenal.

Abolitionist John Brown led the famous raid in 1859 to liberate slaves, and was hanged for his role in the plot.

At midnight they headed toward the arsenal, cutting telegraph wires and taking sixty hostages on their way. The hostage Patrick Higgins escaped and alerted the town. Ironically, the first fatality was a free black man, Heyward Shepherd, who wandered into the area and was shot when trying to flee.

Late Monday morning one hundred marines, led by Robert E. Lee, attacked the arsenal. Brown and his men retreated to the engine house, a small brick building on the arsenal grounds. Within a day the marines captured the engine house, and John Brown's raid at Harpers Ferry was over. Ten men had died in the battle, including Brown's sons, Oliver and Watson.

Marines break down the Armory door at Harpers Ferry, behind which John Brown and his men hide.

Only five slaves were freed as a result of the incident. They had been owned by the mayor of Harpers Ferry, who was slain in the raid. His will ensured their freedom.

John Brown was tried and found guilty of treason, first-degree murder, and conspiracy for advising slaves and others to rebel. On December 2, 1859, Brown was hanged. Six other raiders were also tried for treason and were executed.

John Brown's raid did not accomplish what he had hoped it would, but it did further the abolitionists' cause by making more people aware of it. It also angered people who supported slavery and helped push the nation toward war. On the day of his death, Brown wrote, "I, John Brown am now quite certain that the crimes of this guilty land: will never be purged away: but with Blood. I had as I now think: vainly flattered myself that without very much bloodshed, it might be done."

Brown was right. A sea of blood would be spilled before slavery came to an end. In fact, more Americans died in the Civil War than in all other U.S. wars combined, up to the twenty-first century.

THE CIVIL WAR AND A NEW STATE

In 1861 eleven Southern states seceded (removed themselves) from the Union and formed the Confederate States of America. It was the beginning of the Civil War.

When western Virginians learned that the state of Virginia had voted to secede, they held mass protest meetings and proceeded to create their own state. Delegates from the western counties met at Wheeling on June 11, 1861. There they formed the Restored Government of Virginia, with Francis H. Pierpont as governor. Pierpont's first act was to ask President Abraham Lincoln for military support.

LIVING THROUGH THE CIVIL WAR

Many western Virginians found themselves caught in the middle of the Civil War, facing divided families and loyalties. The diary of the French and Creek teenager Sirene Bunton illustrates the tensions of the era. Though living in what was still part of Virginia (a state that seceded), most people Bunton knew were sympathetic to the Union cause. But there were always exceptions, and Bunton's brother-in-law, Fenton Payne, was one. "To think one of our family is a traitor to our country," Sirene lamented in June 1863.

Payne was a Confederate sympathizer who paid for his beliefs with his life. Despite her Union loyalties, Bunton was sorry about Payne's death: "July 3, 1863. Some dreadful news if true. Fenton Payne and Skid Ferril were killed by our men. They were going to Dixie, but they have gone to their account. I sincerely pity Sister Elsey. I wish I could go and see her. She is left with seven small children and what is to become of them I don't know. . . . It is awful times."

Bunton knew the fear of losing friends and loved ones to the fight. Her three brothers fought with Union forces, and the eldest, Birney, died in the war. Sometimes that fear overwhelmed the fifteen-year-old: "July 6, 1863. All the troops left town last night at nine o'clock for Webster. I expect the citizens of Buchanan are badly frightened now. The [Confederates] surrounded our [troops] at Beverly, took them prisoners, and then killed them in cold blood . . . . The rebels are perfect savages to kill men in that way. I hope they will get their pay for it before they get out of West Virginia."

When that was granted, it made the Restored Government at Wheeling the legal government of Virginia. In October 1861 people of the western counties voted overwhelmingly to form a new state. Two years later West Virginia became the nation's thirty-fifth state.

West Virginia was the site of many Civil War battles. The eastern panhandle bore much of the fighting. The town of Romney changed hands fifty-six times. Conflicting loyalties split families and friendships. It has been estimated that West Virginia contributed 28,000 to 36,000 soldiers to the Union army and 9,000 to 12,000 to the Confederate army.

A STATE OF INDUSTRY

After the war West Virginia began to prosper. Railroads were built to support the lumber and coal industries. The railroads then stimulated those industries, which in turn increased the need for coal. Soon, coal became king.

The mining life was difficult. Booker T. Washington, a former slave who would later found the Tuskegee Institute, moved to West Virginia right after the war. He worked many jobs in Malden, West Virginia, but found coal mining the most grueling. He wrote, "It was a very hard job to get one's skin clean after the day's work was over. . . . I do not believe that one ever experiences anywhere else such darkness as he does in a coal-mine. . . . I many times found myself lost in the mine.

Iron pot cars hold loads of coal at a railroad stop in West Virginia.

To add to the horror of being lost, sometimes my light would go out and then, if I did not happen to have a match, I would wander about in the darkness until by chance I found some one to give me a light."

Mining was not only hard and dirty, it was also dangerous. When breathed, coal dust collects in a miner's lungs and causes a deadly disease called black lung. Sometimes poisonous gases also build up in the mines, causing explosions that kill hundreds of miners. In the early 1900s more coal miners died on the job in West Virginia than in any other state in the country.

Mary Behner helped miners and their families at Scotts Run, a group of coal camps near Morgantown in the northern part of the state. In her diary she described how cheap life was in the 1930s coal camps. After one explosion she wrote, "There was little we could do at The Shack but pacify the crowds that came along to learn of the progress the rescue crews were making. There was a tension among the miners because all knew that it could have easily been the man in their family. Crowds remained at the mouth of the mine for hours in hopes the bodies would be recovered alive. Many of the wives of the rescue crew waited for fear something might happen to them while working, for there was news that another explosion might occur any moment."

This boy worked at the Turkey Knob Mine in 1908 as a tipple boy whose job it was to unload the coal cars by tipping them over.

THE POWER OF BLACK GOLD

With a railroad system built in West Virginia and the already known fact that there was a lot of coal in the state, much of the state's land was slowly bought up by investors who were anxious to get in and make money on so-called black gold—coal. By the late nineteenth and early twentieth centuries a large amount of West Virginia real estate was owned by coal companies. Oftentimes, the coal companies talked local citizens into selling their land, or else they found ways to force West Virginians to turn their land over to them. Some local people thought the prices that the coal mine owners were offering them were a financial windfall. They had no idea how much their land (and the resources hidden under the ground) were really worth.

It took little time for coal companies to become powerful enough to control whole communities. Soon miners who worked in the mines and lived in the area were paying very high prices for food from company-owned stores and were forced to rent houses at unusually high rates because the coal companies owned them and could demand whatever prices they wanted. There was no competition. The coal companies owned everything in these communities, from stores to churches. Miners were kept in debt by having to pay high prices in order to live there and high interest when they had to borrow money or buy things on credit. Most miners were paid not in money but in script, a form of money the mine owners created. Script could only be used in company stores, so miners had no choice but to spend their wages there. One such town was Twin Branch (right), owned by coal mine operator and owner Henry Ford.

People came from many part of the state, from all over the nation, and even from as far away as Europe to work in the mines. They came because they thought they could earn a lot of money. They knew the work was hard, but that did not bother them. Many of these people became disillusioned, though, after performing many months of back-breaking work and still having no money in their savings accounts. Even with the creation of unions, these miners had to fight for their right to make a decent living. There might be a lot of coal in West Virginia, but getting it out of the ground continues to take its toll on miners.

Although there was money to be made in coal mining, it was not the miner who reaped the rewards, but rather the owners of the mines. The only time Mary Behner saw coal miners and their families wearing reasonably new clothes was at funerals—often the funerals of mine-accident victims.

Many West Virginia coal miners thought that by banding together, they could change their poor working conditions. In 1902 they joined a workers' organization, or union, called the United Mine Workers of America (UMWA). To get what they wanted, they agreed among themselves to stop working, or go out on strike.

Mining companies were angered by the strikes. They forced new employees to sign papers agreeing not to join the union and hired guards to prevent union organizers from talking with miners. Miners who did join the UMWA were sometimes beaten up by company guards or locked out of their homes, which were usually owned by the coal mining companies. Still, by 1920, 45,000 West Virginia miners belonged to the UMWA.

Coal was not the only industry growing in West Virginia. During World War I Germany and the United States were on opposite sides of the conflict, so chemicals could not be imported from Germany, as they traditionally had been. Instead, the Kanawha Valley, with its plentiful resources, including salt, became the site of many chemical plants. The federal government constructed a high explosives plant at Nitro and a mustard gas plant at Belle. Nitro, a town of about 25,000 people and 3,400 buildings, sprang up almost overnight in 1918.

Fanny Zerbe, who saw it all happen, wrote, "Gone were the green fields, the quiet days, and the beauty and serenity of life. In their place there had appeared overnight the dirt, the noise, and the ugliness of life. The fields became streets of cement pavements and asphalt roads over which thousands of cars and thousands of pairs of feet passed daily. A miracle had happened.

Overnight the few farms had been made into a city. . . . An impossibility had occurred."

The prosperity that came with these industries was short-lived. In 1929 the Great Depression hit. Across the country banks failed, businesses closed, and millions of workers lost their jobs.

The Mountain State suffered even more than the rest of the country. The percentage of people without jobs was higher in West Virginia than in most other states. The state's UMWA membership dwindled to one thousand. More than 80,000 West Virginia miners were unemployed.

To help West Virginians, the U.S. government created new jobs. Workers were hired to clear hiking paths through the state's forests. Some people were able to become farmers through one government program aimed at helping the beleaguered people living in the Scotts Run coal camps.

Civilian Conservation Corps workers plant trees on a West Virginia hill.

JOHN HARDY

A hundred years ago West Virginia could be a rough and violent place. This song is based on the true story of John Hardy, who was executed for murder on January 19, 1894.

John Hardy stood at the gambling table.
Didn't have no interest in the game.
Up stepped a yellow gal and threw a dollar down,
Said, "John Hardy's playing in my name."

John Hardy took that yellow gal's money,
And then he began to play.
Said, "The man that wins my yellow gal's dollar,
I'll lay him in his lonesome grave."

John Hardy drew to a four-card straight,
And the cowboy drew to a pair.
John failed to catch and the cowboy won,
And he left him sitting dead in his chair.

John started to catch that east-bound train,
So dark he could not see.
Up stepped the police and took him by the arm,
Said, "Johnny, come and go with me."

John Hardy's father came to see him,
Come for to go his bail.
No bail was allowed for a murdering man,
So they shoved John Hardy back in jail.

They took John Hardy to the hanging ground,
And hung him there to die,
And the very last words I heard him say
Were, "My forty-four never told a lie."

"I've been to the east and I've been to the west,
I've traveled this whole world around.
I've been to the river and I've been baptized,
And now I'm on my hanging ground."

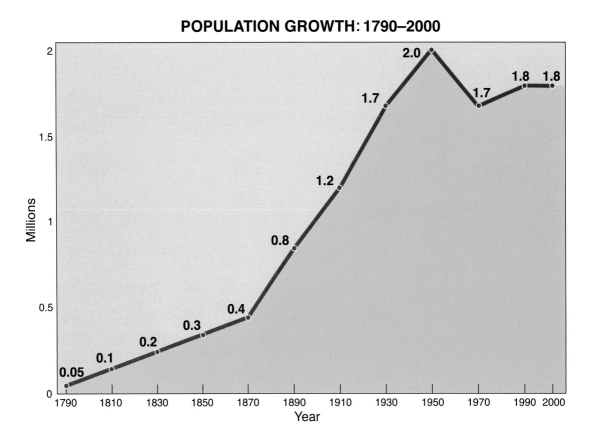

POPULATION GROWTH: 1790–2000

This project meant a new life for many. People traded huts built on slag heaps—mounds of mining waste—for white cottages with gardens. They grew their own food, so their diet was more healthful. And farming offered them a chance to earn a living on their own, escaping the boom-and-bust life of a coal camp.

The journalist William E. Brooks wrote that this new community offered people the chance to "face to the sky instead of to the earth, to watch the long summer wane, and the color come on the mountains, and the snow fall and pass, and the redbud turn the hills to new splendor and the dogwood fleck them with white, instead of being shut away among the slag pile down in one of the 'hallows.' "

Coal continues to be an important industry in West Virginia. While changes have made coal mining safer, it is still the most dangerous industrial job. One of the greatest disasters occurred in 1907 at the Monongah #8 mine, when more than three hundred people lost their lives in a mine explosion. And more recently, in 2006, the whole nation watched on television, hoping that the trapped miners in Tallmansville would be rescued from the Sago Mine.

Even when not directly connected to the industry, some West Virginians have suffered from the coal mining process. On February 26, 1972, after several days of hard rain, a dam holding back mine waste gave way, creating a 30-foot-high wave of 30 million gallons of water. It rushed through the valley of Buffalo Creek in Logan County, wiping out sixteen small communities along the way and killing at least 125 people.

Despite the problems inherent in the coal industry, it remains an important source of income for many residents of the state. That income, however, is not very high. Overall, West Virginia ranks third lowest of all states in per capita income and last in median household income. On the positive side West Virginia's unemployment rate in 2006 was at its lowest point for the past decade.

Another extensive resource is the state's forests. Over 80 percent of West Virginia is covered in forest. This makes the natural surroundings attractive to a growing tourist industry and a major focus for the state's residents. Environmental issues are important and are reflected in the courses of study offered in West Virginia's forty-three universities and colleges. West Virginian students learn how to care for and study their natural environment. Unfortunately, there is a trend among the younger generations to leave the state to search for jobs, not because they want to get away, but rather because there are not enough jobs for them to hold.

West Virginia's natural beauty attracts many tourists.

The natural beauty, the low cost of living, and for many West Virginians the slow pace of everyday life is not enough to put food on the table.

The economy seems to be on everyone's mind. Right before the midterm elections in 2006, a majority of people in West Virginia stated that they considered the economy the most important issue to be addressed. One way some West Virginians have decided to face the economic challenges is to create innovative programs. One program in particular involves researchers at many West Virginia colleges and universities, who are able to work with West Virginia industries to create more efficient, more effective, and more environmentally friendly work practices to help the state compete in the global marketplace. This program, called Industries of the Future—West Virginia, has set up a network to pair educational research with industrial experience.

Other groups are working with teachers, helping them to instill the importance of the basic skills of reading, science, and math in elementary and secondary students. College scholarship programs have also been established to encourage students to further their education after graduating from high school. With working toward improving the state economy as its goal, the West Virginia government has also created a commission to study how to bring new industries, such as those involved with high technologies, to the state.

West Virginia is one of the most beautiful states in the Union. The state's citizens are working hard to keep it that way and to provide the means for its residents to continue to enjoy the good life that the Mountain State offers.

Chapter Three

Proud Mountaineers

West Virginians are often very proud to be from the Mountain State. This can be seen in Muriel Miller Dressler's writing, which was published in 1969.

> "I am Appalachia! In my veins
> Runs Fierce Mountain pride: the hill-fed streams
> Of Passion: and, stranger, you don't know me!"

SMALL TOWNS

Unlike most states in the United States, the majority of the people in West Virginia live in rural areas. (Only Vermont is more rural.) Many hollows, as the state's smallest communities are called, began as small timber and coal-mining camps. Unlike most other American industries, which thrive in metropolitan areas, West Virginia's mining industry thrives in the countryside.

Even West Virginia's cities do not resemble cities in other states, because they do not have large populations. No metropolitan area in the state has more than 60,000 people.

West Virginians take great pride in their state and lay claim to holding the largest percentage of American ancestry in the United States.

It is the beauty of Appalachia and the promise of jobs that brought many people to West Virginia. It is that same beauty that keeps people here and brings others back time and again to enjoy it.

MOUNTAIN STATE HERITAGE

Early immigrants to West Virginia were poor, hardworking people. They came for the natural resources found in the state. Farmers found rich soil in the valleys. Hunters found plenty of deer and other game. Everyone found a place where independence and freedom were honored. These early settlers were proud that the rugged terrain did not get the better of them.

Most early settlers came from Germany or the British Isles. The Appalachian hills reminded them of where they had been born. Today, travelers sometimes have similar reactions. One Scottish visitor to the Mountain State Arts and Crafts Fair in Ripley smiled as he looked at the surrounding peaks. "With the mist on these mountains, it feels like I'm home," he said.

After the Civil War thousands of Italian, Russian, Polish, and Hungarian immigrants came to West Virginia to work in the coal, logging, and railroad industries. Many African Americans seeking jobs also arrived from southern states.

Since the early twentieth century, however, few immigrants from foreign countries have settled in West Virginia. Consequently, almost all Mountaineers today were born in the United States. About 3.2 percent of West Virginians are African American, and 0.8 percent are Hispanic. Only about 1,600 Native Americans and a small number of Asians live in West Virginia.

Many ethnic groups celebrate their heritage with festivals. Every year in late August or early September the West Virginia Italian Heritage Festival is held in Clarksburg. Singers, dancers, and puppeteers dressed in colorful costumes provide entertainment. There is also plenty of great Italian food, such as calzones—folded and cheese-filled pizza dough—for hungry visitors to enjoy.

Many West Virginians can trace their ancestry to people living in the state during its frontier days. Back then villages were places for extended families to gather. Annual clan reunions are still popular in the state. Some get-togethers attract thousands of loosely related people. The Lilly family reunion is a major event in Flat Top every year. "The Lillys are extremely proud of their heritage, what they've accom-

West Virginia has seen an increase in population since 2000 with an average growth of 0.5 percent by 2005.

plished and who they were," said Daniel Lilly, who is a sixth-generation descendant of the first Lilly pioneers who settled in Flat Top in 1732. After living in Rhode Island for twenty-one years, Daniel Lilly decided to move back home. "We all want to go back to our roots," he said. "Heritage is important because the future of our world is based on our past." In recent years the reunion's attendance has dwindled. In its heyday in the 1930s as many as 75,000 people came to the Flat Top get-together. In 2006 the Lillys celebrated their seventy-seventh reunion in a park named in their honor, the Lilly Reunion Memorial Park.

POPULATION DENSITY

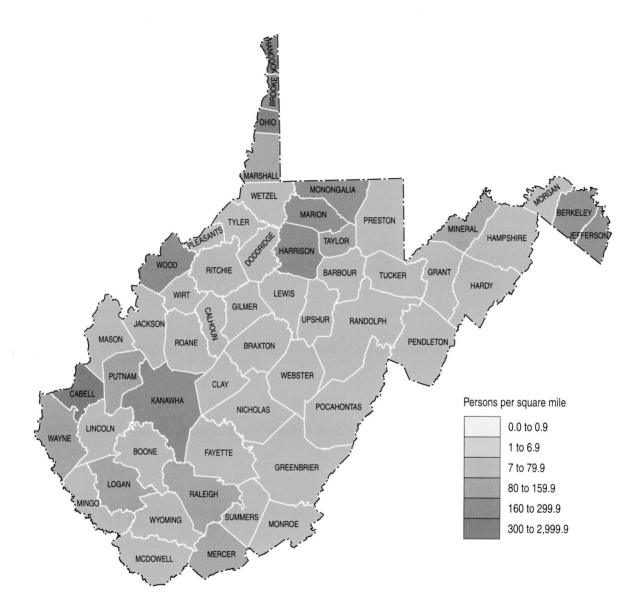

Persons per square mile

0.0 to 0.9

1 to 6.9

7 to 79.9

80 to 159.9

160 to 299.9

300 to 2,999.9

CHASING AWAY WINTER

Tucked away in West Virginia's Allegheny Mountains, a bit of Switzerland thrives. Goat bleats and a babbling creek are the loudest sounds in Helvetia. But as longtime resident and the proprietor of the Beekeeper Inn, Eleanor Mailloux, likes to say, "There are occasional bursts of activity here."

Fasnacht is an old Swiss ritual Helvetians observe every year. It is celebrated one Saturday each February with a Swiss feast and foot-tapping Appalachian music. The townspeople and visitors wear costumes to a masked ball. The scarier the costume the better, because the idea is to drive away the snow, ice, and cold winds. At the end of the day a life-size figure stuffed with hay and firecrackers representing Old Man Winter is brought out. It is burned in a bonfire to make way for spring.

Just like the seasons, Fasnacht comes around every year, but Helvetia always remains the same. Its residents like it that way. "We're all in favor of progress, if you don't make any changes," said Mailloux.

Often, members of the same family stay in one West Virginia town for generations. There is a story about a West Virginia doctor who was visiting out of state and met a woman whose sister-in-law lived in the Appalachian community of Union. "I bet her name is Wikel," said the doctor. The surprised woman said it was and asked the doctor how he knew. "Well, from Union, it had to be either Wikel, or Parker, or Pence," he replied.

The Augusta Heritage Center at Davis and Elkins College in Randolph County is keeping the art and music produced by Appalachia's early settlers alive. Bluegrass, a type of country music, has its origins in Appalachian culture. Appalachian arts and crafts are made from natural resources such as wood, glass, and clay. Most works are made to be used—furniture, quilts, jars, and clay pots.

The Augusta Heritage center connects Appalachian craftspeople, artists, musicians, and dancers with people eager to carry on these rich traditions. Students can learn wood carving, basket making, glassblowing, quilting, and even clogging, a king of tap dancing with heavy wooden shoes. Musicians learn how to play the fiddle or dulcimer, a sweet-sounding stringed instrument that looks a little like a cross between a harp and a guitar. The center provides a common ground on which people of many backgrounds can meet.

Quilt making is a popular tradition in West Virginia.

Basket making is one of the oldest crafts in the nation. The art is continued today in West Virginia.

HILLBILLY IMAGE

Most West Virginians bristle at the prejudiced view some outsiders have of them. Too often, they are characterized as uneducated and unsophisticated. They are called hillbillies, a derogatory term.

It's not certain why the infamous battle between a Kentucky family, the McCoys, and a West Virginia family, the Hatfields, started. But it captured the attention of the nation and helped perpetuate the hillbilly image of mountain folk. Ignored is the fact that some of the Hatfields ended up wealthy and respected members of their community. Henry Drury Hatfield became a senator and later governor of the state of West Virginia. The Matewan police chief Sid Hatfield became a folk hero who defended the rights of impoverished and exploited coal miners in the early twentieth century.

The Hatfields and McCoys enjoy a friendly game of tug-of-war at their reunion in 2000.

At least one West Virginian has embraced the title of hillbilly. In the 1950s Jim Comstock founded the *West Virginia Hillbilly,* "a newspaper for people who can't read, edited by an editor who can't edit." Comstock maintained that what West Virginia needed was "a cheap, unsophisticated country weekly to buck it up, and say some kind words about it now and then, and wrap up its history and colorful lore, and spank it when it gets ugly." The feisty editor took on such issues as bigotry, corruption, discrimination, and greed with help from Ma, Pa, and Fiddlin' Clyde, a fictional hillbilly family whose ignorance served to enlighten readers. Despite the Richwood publication's down-home humor, it was declared "sophisticated" by *Saturday Review* magazine. Comstock demanded a retraction.

Comstock's other accomplishments include preserving a steam railroad, building a hospital, saving the home of the author Pearl S. Buck, creating an annual Past 80 Party for "People with No Quittin' Sense at All," and encouraging everyone to eat ramps.

FRIED RAMPS

Spring in Appalachia brings sweet-smelling flowers and just plain smelly ramps. Ramps are wild leeks, which are related to onions. They grow in West Virginia's mountains between April and June. Families get together and fry up some ramps along a stream or at home. All over the state there are ramp festivals, the most famous being Richwood's Feast of the Ramson.

The late Jim Comstock, the longtime editor of *West Virginia Hillbilly* newspaper, once said about his favorite delicacy, "One of the nice things about ramps—maybe the only nice thing—is that one who eats them can't smell another who had, and that one thing makes a town better to live in when everybody (almost) turns out and eats the stinkers."

Ask an adult to help you make fried ramps. If you don't happen to live in West Virginia, you can substitute leeks or green onions.

1. Wash ramps well and cut off roots.
2. Cut ramps into thirds.
3. Cook bacon in a large skillet and put aside.
4. Add the cut ramps to the bacon grease, and cook until tender.
5. Crumble the bacon and add to the ramps.

Serve with brown beans, corn bread, and cola or root beer.

ETHNIC WEST VIRGINIA

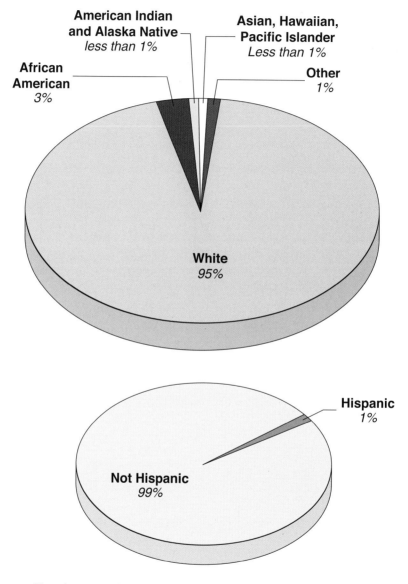

Note: A person of Cuban, Mexican, Puerto Rican, South or Central American, or other Spanish culture or origin, regardless of race, is defined as Hispanic.

Although West Virginia has one of the fewest immigrants of any state, it has welcomed a diverse group of people looking for new homes over the years. As of 2006, 1 percent of West Virginia's population was born in such countries as China, India, Vietnam, the Philippines, Russia, Pakistan, Mexico, Nigeria, Korea, Iran, Germany, and Colombia, just to name a few.

The diversity of the state's population can also be seen in communities that have concentrations of different ethnic groups, whether they are made up of recent immigrants or longtime residents. For example, in the panhandle area, in Berkeley Springs, there is a museum dedicated to the Hungarian culture as well as a Hungarian Freedom Fighters Federation, which preserves and promotes Hungarian heritage.

In the western part of the state, in Metro Valley, a community of about one thousand Asian Indians, enjoys the India Heritage Fair each May, along with other ethnic fairs. And each summer in Wayne, Native Americans gather for a celebration of ceremonial dance and remembrance at a traditional powwow.

Although most West Virginians have assimilated into mainstream American culture, the people of this state have found ways to celebrate and retain their cultural history.

Chapter Four

Governing the Mountain State

Forty years ago Cecil H. Underwood became West Virginia's youngest governor. He served for two terms. In 1996, at age seventy-four, Underwood was elected again. This time, he became the state's oldest governor.

In his inaugural address he remarked on how times have changed, yet how many of the state's problems remain the same. According to Underwood, too much of the state's politics has been built on conflict and division—labor versus management, urban versus rural, north versus south, and east versus west. Conflict has made for a lively political scene, but consensus has been best for solving the most difficult problems, he said.

In 2006 Joe Manchin was West Virginia's governor—a popular one, too, receiving the highest approval rating of all other state governors. However, even Manchin faces challenges similar to the ones that Underwood tried to solve. These include issues such as mine safety, employment, and the economy.

West Virginia's state capitol is located in Charleston, and houses the state's legislature.

Joe Manchin is West Virginia's thirty-fourth governor. He strives to provide West Virginia residents with a strong economy, health care, and education for its young.

Like the federal system, West Virginia has three branches of government: executive, legislative, and judicial.

Executive

The governor is the state's chief executive. He or she appoints many officials and proposes the state budget, which the state legislature then must agree to. A governor may veto (reject) laws or parts of laws passed by the state legislature. But the legislature can override a veto by a majority vote in both houses.

Other elected executive officials are the secretary of state, auditor, treasurer, attorney general, and commissioner of agriculture. Like the governor, all are elected for four-year terms. There is no lieutenant governor in West Virginia. If a governor dies or is too sick to govern, the office is filled by the president of the state senate until a new governor can be elected.

Legislative

The legislature makes new laws and changes old ones. Legislators argue about proposed laws, called bills. When both the state senate and the house of delegates agree to a bill, it is sent to the governor. If the governor signs the bill, it becomes law. The thirty-four state senators are elected for four-year terms. The one hundred members of the house of delegates are elected for two-year terms.

Judicial

West Virginia's court system has three levels. The highest is the Supreme Court of Appeals. It has five justices, who are elected for twelve-year terms. Most of the cases heard by the Supreme Court are appeals from lower courts. The Supreme Court also rules on whether the actions of the executive and legislative branches are constitutional.

The state's major trail courts are called circuit courts. Circuit judges are elected to eight-year terms. The number of judges in each circuit varies from one to seven, depending on the size of the population it serves. Crimes that can be punished by long prison sentences must be tried in circuit courts. At the lowest level are magistrate and municipal courts. Magistrates can decide civil suits involving up to $5,000. Municipal courts deal with violations of city laws. The state also has family law masters, appointed by the governor, who deal with such family matters as divorce, adoption, and child-support payments.

The West Virginia legislature meet in the capitol's house chamber.

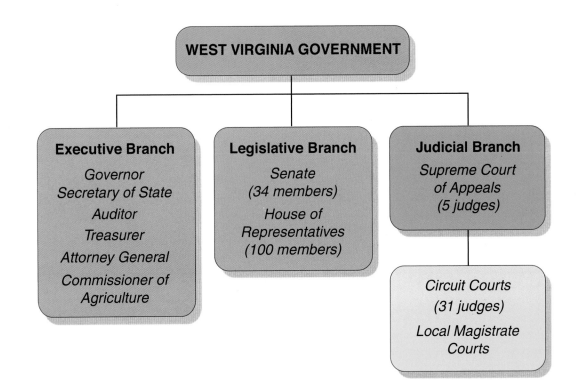

WEST VIRGINIA GOVERNMENT

Executive Branch

Governor
Secretary of State
Auditor
Treasurer
Attorney General
Commissioner of Agriculture

Legislative Branch

Senate
(34 members)

House of Representatives
(100 members)

Judicial Branch

Supreme Court of Appeals
(5 judges)

Circuit Courts
(31 judges)

Local Magistrate Courts

MINE SAFETY BILL, 2006

In response to the Sago Mine disaster of January 2, 2006, during which an explosion trapped thirteen miners for two days, with only one miner rescued alive, the West Virginia legislature passed a bill that created a Mine and Industrial Accident Rapid Response System. This bill required improvements in communications during emergencies at mines, one of the problems that occurred during this disaster.

Although this bill does not solve all the safety issues that have been reported concerning the Sago Mine explosion, it does provide steps toward improving the safety of miners. The bill was introduced to the West Virginia State Senate on January 23, three weeks after the Sago Mine accident.

Governor Manchin hands out copies of the mine safety bill to a family of a mine fire victim in January 2006.

On that same day the bill was read, voted on, and approved by the Senate. On that same day the bill was sent to the West Virginia State House of Representatives. The action in the House was as swift as it had been in the Senate. The representatives also approved the bill on January 23. The bill was sent to the governor on January 24. Governor Manchin signed the bill on January 26, just three days after the bill had first been introduced to the legislature, making it one of the fastest-moving bills to be approved by all three branches of government.

WEST VIRGINIA BY COUNTY

West Virginia's Department of Education "is committed to providing all West Virginia children with skills that will enable them to compete in a fiercely competitive global world."

Schools and education are important to West Virginians. Traditionally, small schools served local communities. However, this meant that state funds were scattered among many small schools, limiting the funds available for any one school. Consolidating several schools under one roof and abandoning smaller school buildings is one way communities are making their schools better equipped. Consolidated schools can offer students more resources. For instance, they might be able to offer advanced science classes or three foreign languages instead of just one. While consolidation makes a lot of sense in urban areas, it sometimes has unfortunate consequences in rural ones.

For many rural communities separated by steep ridges and deep valleys, schools are the place to gather. They are used by everyone in town, not just by students. In many cases the schools provide a place to hold meetings and festivals, to stage theater, and to play basketball. Schools are also a big source of pride. Rural residents come to the school to cheer on local sports teams and meet with neighbors. If the schools are shut down, the communities lose their center and focus.

The issue has caused fierce debate in most of the state's rural communities. "You always hear a lot about this issue," said Pam Ramsey, a newspaper editor in Beckley. Despite the dissent from rural residents, many county school systems have decided that consolidation is worth it. Still, many people feel their communities have lost a lot, while students have gained.

Chapter Five
Working Together

For a long time West Virginians struggled with high unemployment rates and poverty. But in recent years the tide has been slowly turning. The economy is showing some signs of improvement as West Virginians search for new technologies, attract new types of businesses, and create new educational programs to ensure a well-trained workforce.

One of the mainstays of West Virginia's economy for many years has been mining. It is no wonder. Of the fifty-five counties in West Virginia, coal is found in fifty-three of them. The West Virginia mountains hold about 4 percent of the world's coal supply. In 2005 West Virginians mined about 159 million tons of coal. In all, about 40,000 West Virginians work for the coal industry. Natural gas, oil, and salt are also mined in West Virginia.

Another industry that employs many West Virginians is manufacturing. In 2006 almost 61,400 people in the state worked for some type of manufacturing business. Some of the largest employers in the state include manufacturers who make metals, chemicals, wood products, processed foods, plastic and rubber products, computers and electronic equipment, and transportation equipment.

One of West Virginia's most bountiful natural resources is coal.

LEAVING DEHUE

Coal mining built Dehue Hollow. Now it has destroyed it.

"This used to be the prettiest camp around," said Lena Adkins on the last night she slept in the house she had called home for forty-two years.

"My son lives up in Delaware, and he says, 'Mom, I just love to come home and sit in the old porch swing.' He was here two weeks ago, and he just couldn't get over the fact that it's the last time he'll see this place."

As in other hollows, mining companies forced residents out. Then, waste from the mining operations buried the towns.

In the 1920s the Youngstown Mine Corporation built houses for its workers, who in turn paid rent to the company. Delores Riggs Davis of Kirtland, Ohio, described the town's heyday as a magical time, when people from many different cultures came together. "Some came directly from Ellis Island to find work in Dehue," said Davis. Ellis Island is where many immigrants first landed when they arrived from Europe by boat. Now Dehue, like many other small towns across West Virginia, is gone.

Glassmaking has a long history in West Virginia. The state has been home to more than five hundred glass factories. Blenko Glass Company in Milton is famous for producing fine stained glass. Blenko glassmakers must train for years to produce this material correctly.

Manufacturing employs more than 60,000 West Virginians.

Blenko Glass can be found in many of the nation's best-known churches, such as the Washington National Cathedral in Washington, D.C., and the Cathedral of Saint John the Divine in New York City. Overall, manufacturing represents 11 percent of West Virginia's gross state product.

A glass worker shapes a vase at Blenko Glass.

EARNING A LIVING

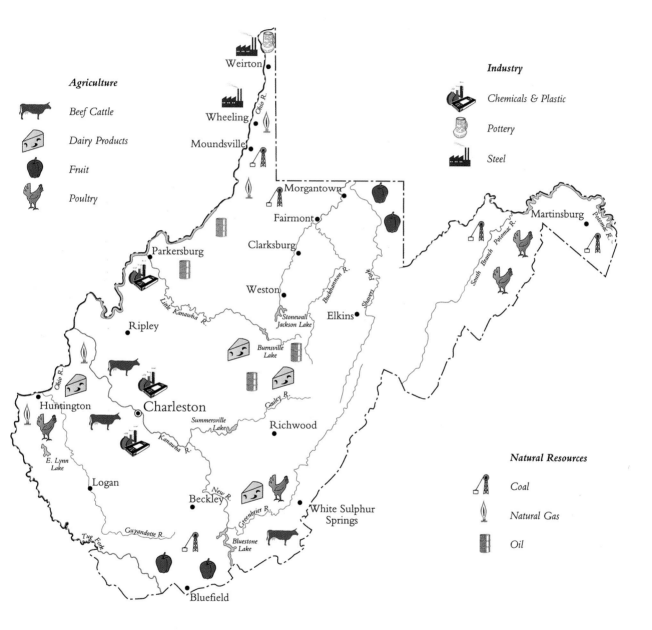

Agriculture

Beef Cattle

Dairy Products

Fruit

Poultry

Industry

Chemicals & Plastic

Pottery

Steel

Natural Resources

Coal

Natural Gas

Oil

Weirton

Wheeling

Moundsville

Morgantown

Fairmont

Clarksburg

Martinsburg

Parkersburg

Weston

Elkins

Ripley

Stonewall
Jackson Lake

Burnsville
Lake

Huntington

Charleston

Summersville
Lake

Richwood

Logan

Beckley

White Sulphur
Springs

Bluestone
Lake

E. Lynn
Lake

Bluefield

Ohio R.

Little Kanawha R.

Kanawha R.

New R.

Greenbrier R.

Guyandotte R.

Tug Fork

Gauley R.

Buckhannon R.

Shavers Fork

South Branch Potomac R.

Potomac R.

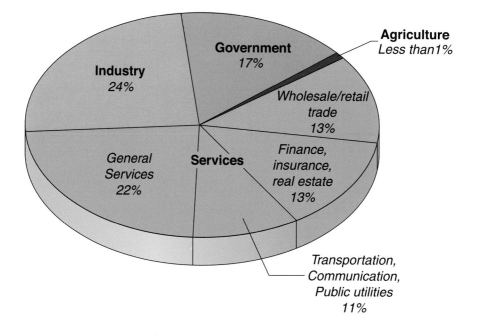

2004 GROSS STATE PRODUCT: $50 Million

Government 17%

Agriculture Less than 1%

Industry 24%

Wholesale/retail trade 13%

General Services 22%

Services

Finance, insurance, real estate 13%

Transportation, Communication, Public utilities 11%

There is another business that is quickly adding much-needed money to the state's economy—tourism. In the past, traditional industries, although they created much-needed jobs, harmed the state by polluting the air and water, wreaking havoc on its forests, and leaving ugly gouges in once-beautiful mountains. In contrast, tourism does best when the state's natural splendor is preserved.

According to the Wheeling Convention and Visitor's Bureau, travelers to the state spend more than $3.4 billion each year, thus providing more than 40,000 jobs for West Virginians who work in tourist related businesses such as hotels and restaurants. Between 2000 and 2005, travel spending in West Virginia increased by over 11 percent each year, making tourism a steadily growing industry. Biking, canoeing, river-rafting, hiking, hunting, fishing, and camping are all popular reasons that tourists come to the state. People are also attracted by such cultural events as music and art fairs.

In order to serve this growing number of tourists, West Virginia's Department of Education has created a program lovingly referred to as HEAT (Hospitality Education and Training). The education department works with the tourism industry to help educate and train West Virginia's schoolchildren for jobs that serve the growing number of tourists flocking to the state.

West Virginia's tourism industry generates more than $3 billion per year and employs more than 40,000.

Programs offered by HEAT include Travel West Virginia, a course that combines the study of the state's history, geography, and culture with an understanding of marketing. Another program focuses on the culinary arts, so that students can gain entry into the fine-dining industry. There is also a program developed by the American Hotel and Lodging Association Educational Institute through which students learn about hotel management.

These courses are offered on the high school level, but they provide college credit, giving students a head start in obtaining an advanced degree.

To generate interest in these programs, some West Virginia high schools have become involved in national competitions. For instance, in 2005 Greenbrier East High School, which won a state competition, was then eligible to vie for a culinary award at a competition in Orlando, Florida. Its students were able to demonstrate their culinary skills by preparing creative fine-dining meals.

AGRICULTURE

Despite its rural landscape West Virginia does not have much agriculture, because there is little flat land on which to grow produce. But in the eastern panhandle, apples and peaches are popular crops. The state ranks eighth in the country in apple production and fourteenth in peach production. West Virginia farmers were the first to produce Golden Delicious apples.

West Virginia's farmers do not all depend on crops, though. Many farmers raise livestock. In 2005 farmers sold over 88.5 million broilers (chickens), the fifteenth-highest amount of all the states, making chickens the number-one agriculture commodity in West Virginia. Raising cattle was the second-largest agricultural commodity in the state. Other items that are produced on West Virginia's farms include eggs, turkeys, and dairy products.

West Virginia ranks eighth in the nation in apple production.

West Virginia's rolling landscape supports the raising of cattle.

Although West Virginia's unemployment rate is moderate, its poverty rate is one of the highest of the fifty states, at 14.8 percent in 2005. The state ranks lowest of all the states for average family income. Balancing this out a little, at least, is West Virginia's relatively low cost of living.

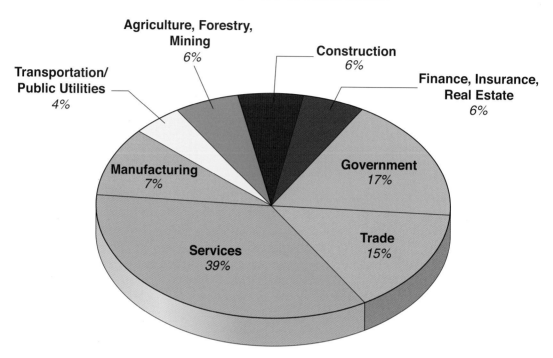

WEST VIRGINIA WORKFORCE

Agriculture, Forestry, Mining
6%

Construction
6%

Finance, Insurance, Real Estate
6%

Transportation/ Public Utilities
4%

Government
17%

Manufacturing
7%

Trade
15%

Services
39%

A CHANCE TO STAY

West Virginia has been called one of the nation's most popular places to be from. The state was one of only seven to lose population between 1980 and 1990. That trend has changed in recent years, but just barely. In 2005 West Virginia ranked forty-fourth of the fifty states in population growth rates.

Most former Mountaineers, as West Virginians are known, left the state to seek jobs elsewhere. There have been two major migrations from the state. In the 1950s mechanization put thousands of coal miners out of work. Most went to northern industrial cities, such as Detroit, Akron, and Cleveland. Then in the mid-1980s the lagging coal industry and a nationwide recession sent many West Virginians south, looking for jobs in places such as Charlotte, North Carolina.

To attract new residents and to keep current ones, West Virginia must provide employment opportunities.

The recent growth of the state's tourism industry has proven how attractive a place West Virginia can be. But if people are to stay in the state, they must have jobs. The state government and business organizations are working hard to attract new industry by promoting the state as a good place to do business. Improving the education and technological skills of today's students will provide better workers for new industries, such as high technology. The new slogan for West Virginia is "Open for Business."

Chapter Six

A Tourist's Dream

It has been a long time coming, but people are finally recognizing how wonderful it is to visit the Mountain State. West Virginia is a place to go rock climbing, white-water rafting, kayaking, hiking, and skiing. It is also a place just to relax and enjoy the beauty of the Appalachians.

Many people have discovered the state since the completion of major highways has made it more accessible. But to really see West Virginia, you need to get off the main highways and onto winding mountain roads.

THE SOUTH

Southern West Virginia used to be a collection of poor coal-mining villages tucked away in mountain hollows. Today it looks very different.

On the north side of Beckley a spiked, bright red roof stands out against the landscape. This is Tamarack, which is known as the Best of West Virginia. In creating Tamarack, the former governor W. Gaston Caperton III envisioned a home for the state's rich cultural heritage. It is a place where jobs, marketing, training, and educational opportunities abound for West Virginia's artists, producers, craftspeople, and farmers.

The Mountain State attracts visitors like this one, climbing a steep rock wall above New River Gorge National River.

"West Virginia Made" textiles, glass, pottery, jewelry, baskets, specialty foods, and souvenirs are for sale at Tamarack. The center also features five craft demonstration studios, a theater presenting films and live performances, gallery exhibits, gardens, and a nature trail.

The West Virginia state park system is one of the most beautiful in the country. Many of its best parks are located along the New River Gorge. In the spring the area is bursting with rhododendron and mountain laurel blooms. Hawks Nest and Grandview State Parks both have spectacular views of the gorge.

New River Gorge National River is one of the most scenic parks in the state.

BRIDGE DAY

"Elvis has left the bridge!" cried the crowd when twenty-nine-year-old Patrick Weldon parachuted off the New River Gorge Bridge dressed in a sequined costume reminiscent of the King of Rock and Roll, Elvis Presley.

Daredevil stunts are just one part of Bridge Day, West Virginia's largest one-day festival. Celebrated on the third Saturday of October, the festival commemorates the completion of the New River Gorge Bridge in 1977. The bridge has the world's second longest single-arch steel span and, at 876 feet above the New River, is the second-highest bridge in the country.

"Thank you, West Virginia!" screamed Chris Stokeley of Houston, Texas, as he dove over the bridge railing. Parachutists and BASE jumpers (BASE stands for Building, Antenna, Span, Earth—the fixed objects from which these jumpers leap) love West Virginia, because the New River Gorge Bridge is one of the few places in the world where they can make a lawful jump.

Beneath the bridge dangle expert rappellers, people who use ropes to descend from the bridge. Resembling spiders weaving a web, they practice their well-honed skills with the breathtaking gorge as a backdrop. Other rappellers are on hand for rescue operations in the gorge if necessary, because this can be a very dangerous sport. Four people have been killed since the first Bridge Day was held in 1980.

In 1996 four hundred parachutists and nineteen rappel teams from fifteen states and Canada attended the event. But today, most people come to Bridge Day just to walk across the 3,030-foot-long bridge. On this one day each year the bridge is closed to traffic and open to pedestrians.

The New River attracts many tourists. Abandoned coal-mining towns, scenic waterfalls, and tall tales told by guides are usually part of a good rafting or canoeing trip.

The once-thriving railroad and mining town of Thurmond can be seen from the New River. Thurmond has a history similar to that of a Wild West town, and its population has dwindled to only a few houses hugging a gorge known as the Grand Canyon of the East. Thurmond's main street isn't a street at all. Instead, it is railroad tracks running parallel to the river, a vivid reminder of what made this community boom and then go bust. The historic Thurmond Depot has been restored and now serves as a visitor's center. Exhibits and period furnishings bring the golden days of railroading back to life. People today no longer visit Thurmond to have wild times at the notorious Dunglen Hotel. Instead, many are mountain bikers just passing through.

At Babcock State Park a mountain trout stream called Glade Creek rushes through a rocky canyon, creating waterfalls as it goes. The Glade Creek Grist Mill has become a favorite with many of the nation's photographers. Reconstructed from portions of old mills from throughout the state, this fully operational mill offers freshly ground cornmeal, buckwheat, and whole-wheat flour to park guests.

Bramwell is near the state's southern border with Virginia. Settled by wealthy coal-mine owners at the end of the nineteenth century, Bramwell was once dubbed "the richest small town in America." It was home to as many as nineteen millionaires, who made their fortunes in the Pocahontas County coalfields. The prosperous Bank of Bramwell was the hub of southern West Virginia's financial network. The bank closed in 1933 in the midst of the Great Depression, and most of Bramwell's wealthy residents left. Today, Bramwell's former Victorian charm has been restored, to the delight of tourists. Some of the old estates have been turned into bed and breakfast inns, and most are part of a tour highlighting the town's heyday.

The Glade Creek Grist Mill is a fully operational mill in Babcock State Park.

At least one southern West Virginia spot has maintained its prosperity and grandeur and still frequently welcomes famous visitors. The Greenbrier Hotel at White Sulphur Springs is one of the last grand, old hotels left in the United States.

The Greenbrier has experienced much of the nation's history. During the Civil War both Union and Confederate troops occupied the hotel. At the beginning of World War II it was used as an internment center for German and Japanese diplomats who were waiting to be traded for American diplomats abroad. Then in September 1942 the hotel was turned into a hospital by the U.S. Army.

The recent revelation of one of the best-kept secrets in the state has added to the hotel's colorful history. The Greenbrier was the sight of a top-secret bunker designed to house the members of the U.S. Congress in the event of a nuclear war. The facility was built under the hotel between 1958 and 1961. The secrecy of the bunker was maintained for more than thirty years, but on May 31, 1992, the *Washington Post* published a story exposing it. The next day the facility began to be phased out. Tours of the bunker are very popular.

THE STATE CAPITAL

West Virginia's largest city is its capital, Charleston. At the center of town, covered in gold leaf, shines the dome of the capitol. Completed in 1932, the building was designed by Cass Gilbert, a renowned architect who also designed the Supreme Court building in Washington, D.C., and the capitols of Minnesota and Arkansas. The dome of West Virginia's capitol is 292 feet high, higher than the dome of the nation's capitol in Washington.

The grounds of the state capitol include the state museum and cultural center, statuary, West Virginia's Memorial Plaza, and governor's mansion.

Also on the capitol grounds is the state museum, which has displays illustrating life in the Mountain State, from its Native-American past to the present. Charleston is also the site of the Avampato Discovery Museum, which has art and science exhibits, a planetarium, and a children's museum.

Each May Charleston hosts the Vandalia Gathering, a celebration of traditional Appalachian music. Visitors listen to the sweet sounds of fiddles, banjos, and mountain dulcimers. The city's best-known festival is held in September, when every boat around seems to be out on the Kanawha for Charleston's regatta. Craft booths and food courts line the riverbanks, and both land and river lovers delight in a spectacular fireworks display.

PLACES TO SEE

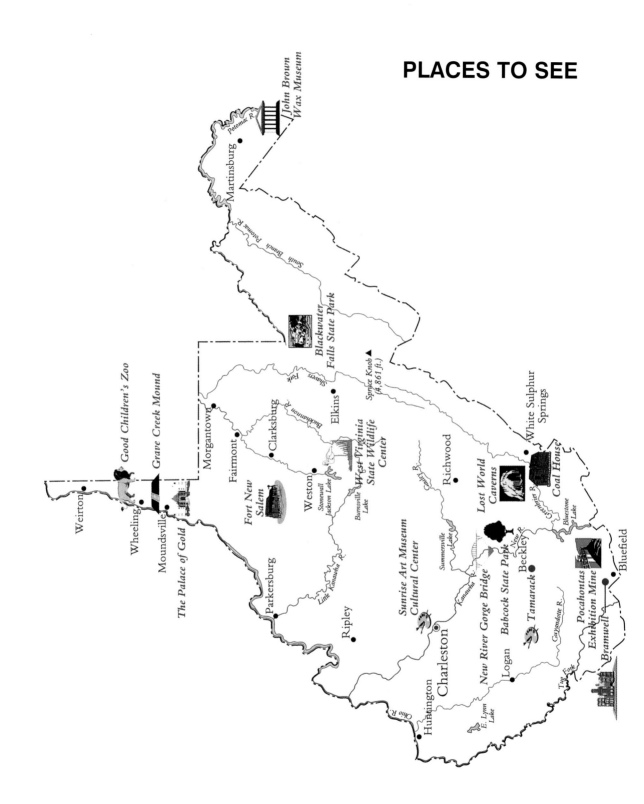

John Brown Wax Museum

Potomac R.

Martinsburg

South Branch Potomac R.

Blackwater Falls State Park

Spruce Knob (4,861 ft.)

Shavers Fork

Good Children's Zoo

Grave Creek Mound

Morgantown

Clarksburg

Elkins

Buckhannon R.

White Sulphur Springs

West Virginia State Wildlife Center

Fairmont

Fort New Salem

Weston

Stonewall Jackson Lake

Burnsville Lake

Richwood

Lost World Caverns

Coal House

Gauley R.

Greenbrier R.

Weirton

Wheeling

Moundsville

The Palace of Gold

Bluestone Lake

Parkersburg

Little Kanawha R.

Summersville Lake

Sunrise Art Museum Cultural Center

New River Gorge Bridge

Babcock State Park

New R.

Beckley

Tamarack

Pocahontas Exhibition Mine

Bluefield

Ripley

Kanawha R.

Logan

Bramwell

Charleston

Guyandotte R.

Huntington

Tug Fork

Ohio R.

E. Lynn Lake

South of Wheeling is Moundsville and the Grave Creek Mound State Park, where modern American archaeology was born. In 1881 Congress gave the Smithsonian Institution $5,000 for the excavation and study of Native-American burial mounds. The first excavation was of the Grave Creek Mound, one of the most famous and certainly the largest of the Adena burial mounds. Constructed between 250 and 150 B.C.E., the mound is 69 feet high and 295 feet across, and contains over 60,000 tons of earth. Excavation of these mounds has unearthed such artifacts as a copper headdress and flint knives. By the time the Smithsonian completed its excavation project in 1890, over two thousand mounds and earthworks had been studied in the eastern United States. About a hundred of these were in the Kanawha Valley.

THE EASTERN PANHANDLE

Only about an hour's drive away from the nation's capital, the eastern panhandle has become part of Washington, D.C.'s, suburban outskirts. Despite increasing urbanization, the area has maintained its natural beauty and early American charm.

Historic sights are scattered throughout the eastern panhandle. Long before the first Europeans discovered its warm waters, Berkeley Springs was already a famous health spa, attracting Native Americans from Canada to the Carolinas. The springs became a favorite of George Washington as early as 1748, but not until 1756 did North America's first public mineral springs resort open there. Heat and pressure deep below Earth's surface cause the springwater to gush out of the ground at a soothing 74 °F.

The stretch of the Alleghenies at the base of the eastern panhandle resembles Canada more than the southern United States. In winter Spruce Knob, West Virginia's highest point, is often unreachable because of ice and snow. In spring and summer mountain bikers and hikers work hard to get to the top. Those who make it are rewarded with a spectacular view. As visitors climb the peak, the thick pine forests give way to more barren, rocky terrain. On top most trees have branches only on one side, because cold winds freeze growth on the other. At Spruce Knob's peak miles of green valleys and rising forests can be seen. Eagles and hawks often soar over the landscape. It is a good place just to sit quietly. "You realize how small a part of the universe you are from up here," said one hiker.

Spruce Knob is West Virginia's tallest peak at 4,863 feet above sea level.

Southwest of Spruce Knob is Seneca Rocks, a sandstone rock formation that looks out of place among the surrounding forested ridges. Bare and dramatic in form, it resembles parts of the southwestern United States. Serious rock climbers test their skills on the 900-foot cliff there.

Seneca Rocks is one of West Virginia's best known landmarks.

THE NATIONAL RADIO ASTRONOMY OBSERVATORY

Sometimes scientists can learn as much from listening as they can from seeing. By listening for sounds in space, the telescopes at the National Radio Astronomy Observatory in Deer Creek Valley can tell scientists all sorts of things about the universe. The telescopes can help answer questions concerning what space is made of, the nature of time, and whether other stars and galaxies exist that we do not know about.

To most people, radio waves just sound like a lot of static. But scientists armed with computers can tell much from what they hear. A change in rhythm or pitch can indicate the location of a planet, moon, or other object in space.

Radio telescopes look like huge satellite dishes. The observatory's newest machine, the Green Bank Telescope, is the largest steerable telescope in the world.

The National Radio Astronomy Observatory is located in rural West Virginia for good reason. The remoteness of Deer Creek Valley and the surrounding mountains protect the sensitive receivers used on the telescopes against unwanted radio interference.

TEN LARGEST CITIES

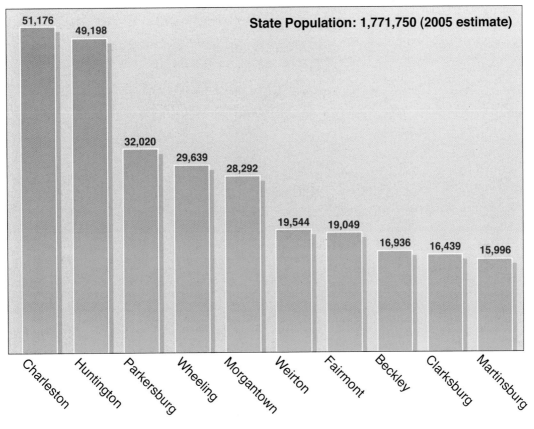

State Population: 1,771,750 (2005 estimate)

Charleston	51,176
Huntington	49,198
Parkersburg	32,020
Wheeling	29,639
Morgantown	28,292
Weirton	19,544
Fairmont	19,049
Beckley	16,936
Clarksburg	16,439
Martinsburg	15,996

At Dolly Sods trails lead hikers through arctic bogs. But visitors must read warning signs and be careful where they walk. During World War II Dolly Sods was used for military exercises, and some live mortar shells are buried in the soil. The forest service continues to clear the area of these hazards, but some shells are still out there. If a hiker happens upon an unexploded shell, he or she is warned not to touch it. While discovering shells is extremely rare, they are occasionally found by hunters and backcountry hikers.

Dolly Sods, at more than 10,000 acres, offers visitors many trails to explore, camp sites, and wildlife.

At Blackwater Falls State Park the six-story-high falls can be seen from several vantage points at the edge of the Blackwater River Gorge. It's a spectacular sight for both first-time visitors and devout fans of this park.

Beautiful scenery and train and logging industry history are all experienced on a trip on the Cass Scenic Railroad. The route takes riders from the old lumber town of Cass to the summit of Bald Knob, the second-highest peak in the state. The train is powered by a specially designed Shay steam locomotive, which was once used to haul logs. Now it takes passengers past breathtaking mountain scenery.

The railroad is the last remaining segment of the massive lumber railroad network that once covered every valley and mountain in Pocahontas County. The sawmills that these railroads supplied with timber made Pocahontas County one of the leading lumber-producing areas in the eastern United States for many years.

Full of history and natural beauty, a sportsman's paradise, and a quiet retreat, West Virginia is truly wild and wonderful. It is a place visitors are happy to find and natives love to return to.

Blackwater Falls drops five stories before rapidly flowing through an 8-mile gorge.

THE FLAG: Adopted in 1929, the state flag features the state seal against a white background with a blue border. At the top of the seal are the words "State of West Virginia." Rhododendron, the state flower, surround the rest of the seal.

THE SEAL: Adopted in 1863, the state seal bears the words "State of West Virginia" and the state motto "Montani Semper Liberi" (Mountaineers Are Always Free). In the center a farmer and a miner stand next to a rock with the date 1863, the year West Virginia became a state. In front of the rock are two rifles, which symbolize the willingness to fight for freedom.

State Survey

Statehood: June 20, 1863

Origin of Name: Western counties of Virginia separated from the state during the Civil War, rather than secede from the Union. Virginia was named for Elizabeth I, the Virgin Queen of England.

Nickname: Mountain State, and unofficially, the Panhandle State

Capital: Charleston

Motto: Montani Semper Liberi (Mountaineers Are Always Free)

Bird: Cardinal

Animal: Black bear

Fish: Brook trout

Flower: Rhododendron

Tree: Sugar maple

Insect: Honeybee

Fruit: Golden Delicious apple

Colors: Gold and blue

Cardinal

Black bear

THE WEST VIRGINIA HILLS

West Virginia has three state songs, but in 1961 the state legislature stated in an official resolution that this was the best known and most widely sung in the state. The words were written in 1879 and set to music in 1885.

Highest Point: 4,863 feet above sea level at Spruce Knob

Lowest Point: 240 feet above sea level along the Potomac River in Harpers Ferry

Area: 24,231 square miles

Greatest Distance North to South: 237 miles

Great Distance East to West: 265 miles

Bordering States: Ohio to the northwest, Pennsylvania and Maryland to the north, Virginia to the east and south, Kentucky to the southwest

Hottest Recorded Temperature: 112 °F at Martinsburg on July 10, 1936, and at Moorefield on August 4, 1930

Coldest Recorded Temperature: –37 °F at Lewisburg on December 30, 1917

Average Annual Precipitation: 44 inches

Major Rivers: Guyandotte, Kanawha, Little Kanawha, Monongahela, New, Ohio, Potomac, Tygart, West Fork

Major Lakes: there are no large natural lakes; artificial reservoirs have been created on the New, Gauley, and Tygart rivers

Trees: beech, cherry, hemlock, hickory, maple, oak, poplar, red spruce, white pine

Wild Plants: aster, azalea, black-eyed Susan, bloodroot, dogwood, goldenrod, hepatica, redbud, rhododendron, white-blossomed hawthorn, wild crab apple

Animals: black bear, bobcat, gray fox, groundhog, mink, opossum, otter, rabbit, raccoon, red fox, skunk, squirrel, white-tailed deer

Fish: bass, bluegill, catfish, crappie, muskellunge, pickerel, trout, walleyed pike

Birds: brown thrasher, cardinal, eagle, falcon, hawk, quail, scarlet tanager, snipe, wood thrush

Hawk

Endangered Animals: American peregrine falcon, bald eagle, club-shell mussel, Cheat mountain salamander, eastern cougar, fanshell, flat-spired three-toothed snail, gray bat, harperella, Indiana bat, James River spiny mussel, northeastern bulrush, northern riffeshell, pink mucket pearly mussel, Virginia big-eared bat, Virginia northern flying squirrel

Endangered Plants: bulrush, harperella, rock cress, running buffalo clover, pogonia, Virginia spiraea

TIMELINE

West Virginia History

c. 1000 B.C.E. The mound-building Adena Indians inhabit the area.

1600 C.E. Iroquois Confederacy tribes hunt in the region.

1669 John Lederer, the first European to see western Virginia, travels to the top of the Blue Ridge.

1671 Englishmen Thomas Batts and Robert Fallam cross the Allegheny Mountains, which helps England claim the Ohio Valley.

1742 John P. Salling and John Howard discover coal on the Coal River.

1754–1755 Frenchmen and Indians defeat British troops led by George Washington and General Edward Braddock during the French and Indian War.

1773 Plans for a fourteenth colony, which would include West Virginia, collapse.

1782 Although the American Revolution has ended, British troops and Native Americans raid Fort Henry at Wheeling.

1788 Charleston is founded.

1788 Daniel Boone settles in the Kanawha Valley.

1815 Natural gas is discovered near Charleston.

1836 B&O (Baltimore and Ohio) Railroad from Chesapeake Bay reaches Harpers Ferry.

1859 John Brown raids the federal arsenal at Harpers Ferry.

1861 Western counties of Virginia refuse to secede from the Union; they form their own government, the Restored Government of Virginia.

1863 West Virginia becomes the thirty-fifth state.

1872 State constitution is ratified.

1890 United Mine Workers of America begins to organize in the state.

1907 Worst mining disaster in U.S. history leaves 362 dead at Monongah.

1919–1921 Labor disputes involving coal miners break out in Logan and Mingo Counties.

1924 West Virginian John W. Davis becomes Democratic presidential nominee, but loses to Calvin Coolidge.

1954 The West Virginia Turnpike opens.

1959 National Radio Astronomy Observatory begins operating at Green Bank.

1968 Explosions and fire in a coal mine in Farmington kill seventy-eight people and lead to new mining safety laws.

1972 Buffalo Creek flood kills more than ten people near Man.

1985 State lottery is established.

1990 West Virginian Kathy Mattea wins a Grammy Award.

1997 Mary Lou Retton is inducted into the International Gymnastics Hall of Fame.

2004 Joe Manchin is elected as West Virginia's thirty-fourth governor.

2005 West Virginia University retires Basketball Hall of Fame legend Jerry West's jersey number 44.

2006 Sago Mine explosion traps thirteen miners. Only one survives.

Agricultural Products: apples, corn, hay, livestock and livestock products (beef, chicken, milk, turkey), peaches, tobacco

Manufactured Products: chemicals, food products, glass products, machinery, pottery, steel

Natural Resources: clay, coal, gravel, limestone, natural gas, petroleum, rock salt, sand

Business and Trade: communication, tourism, transportation

Coal

Feast of the Ramson In April, Richwood and other towns celebrate the ramp, a wild leek that grows between April and June. The Richwood festival features an old-fashioned ramp dinner, as well as arts and crafts, old-time music, and dancing. At the Elkins ramp celebration you can eat ramps fried, boiled, and any other way you can think of at the Ramp Cook-Off.

Blue and Gray Reunion During the first weekend in June in Philippi, actors re-create the first land battle of the Civil War. Other events during this living history weekend include artillery demonstrations and a costumed Civil War ball.

Sternwheel Regatta and River Festival At this June festival in Point Pleasant, you can enjoy sternwheel races, towboat demonstrations, a parade, dancing, and arts-and-crafts displays.

West Virginia State Fair This nine-day fair in Lewisburg in early August draws exhibitors and visitors from throughout the region. Enjoy horse shows, food, livestock competitions, and musical entertainment.

West Virginia Oil and Gas Festival In early September Sistersville celebrates its history as an oil boomtown with a parade, a gas-engine show, a wood-chopping contest, an antique car show, a crafts fair, oil and gas equipment displays, and a fiddling contest.

Civil War Days During the second week of September Gauley Bridge, the site of heavy fighting during the Civil War, honors its past. You can watch a Civil War reenactment staged at Carnifax Ferry Battlefield State Park and also enjoy parades, sporting events, and wood-chopping contests.

Country Roads Festival During the third week of September visitors to Hawks Nest State Park in Ansted kick up their heels to great bluegrass and gospel music and participants in clogging, a form of tap dancing.

Mountaineer Balloon Festival Fall in Morgantown brings this three-day celebration of flight. Watch the launch of dozens of colorful hot-air balloons, and then enjoy music and carnival rides.

West Virginia Italian Heritage Festival This September celebration in Clarksburg honors the state's citizens of Italian descent. Costumed minstrels, singers, dancers, actors, and puppeteers entertain visitors.

Mountain State Forest Festival Highlights of the state's oldest festival, held in Elkins in October, include wood-chopping contests, parades, and jousting. The festival also features crafts, food, and the crowning of the festival's Queen Silvia.

Battle Days For two days in October Point Pleasant remembers the 1774 battle that some historians call the opening exchange of the Revolutionary War. The celebration includes military reenactments; a colonial ball with period costumes, music, and dance; a parade; and an ox roast.

Apple Butter Festival If it's Columbus Day weekend, it's time to savor the apple butter at Berkeley Springs. You can also enjoy the music and crafts, but the emphasis is on food—especially the apple butter simmering in giant kettles over open fires.

Old Tyme Christmas A candlelit walk, caroling, and children's programs during the first two weekends in December help visitors to Harpers Ferry get into the holiday spirit.

STATE STARS

Nnamdi Azikiwe (1904–1996) was the first president of the Republic of Nigeria. He attended Storer College in Harpers Ferry.

Randy Barnes (1966–), born in Charleston, won a silver medal in 1988 and a gold medal in 1996 in the shot put at the Olympics. He holds the outdoor and indoor distance world records in shot put.

Pearl S. Buck (1892–1973), born in Hillsboro, was the third American to receive the Nobel Prize for Literature. She was the daughter of American missionaries and lived in China until 1933. She returned to the United States and lived the rest of her life in West Virginia. She is best known for her novels set in China, especially *The Good Earth*, for which she won a Pulitzer Prize in 1932.

Pearl S. Buck

Robert C. Byrd (1917–   ) was born in North Carolina, but was raised by relatives in West Virginia after his mother died. Byrd has been a leading Democrat in the U.S. Senate since 1959. Byrd entered politics in 1946, serving in the West Virginia House of Delegates, the state senate, and the U.S. House of Representatives, before being elected to the U.S. Senate. He is well known for his mastery of the complex legislative system. As of 2006 Byrd was the longest-serving current member of the U.S. Senate.

Stephen Coonts (1946–), author of the Vietnam War novel *Flight of the Intruder*, was born in Morgantown. He also wrote the best sellers *The Cannibal Queen*, *Final Flight*, *The Minotaur*, *Under Siege*, and *The Red Horseman*. In 2006 Coonts published his twentieth book, *The Traitor*.

George Henry Crumb (1929–), born in Charleston, is a composer known for his innovative use of instrumental and vocal effects, such as hissing, whispering, tongue-clicking, and shouting. His most famous work is *Echoes of Time and the River*, which earned him a Pulitzer Prize in music in 1968.

John W. Davis (1873–1955) was the Democratic candidate for president in 1924, but he lost to Calvin Coolidge. Prior to this, Davis had served in the U.S. House of Representatives and as the U.S. ambassador to Great Britain. He was also the solicitor general in Woodrow Wilson's administration and argued more cases before the Supreme Court than any other attorney in history. Davis was born in Clarksburg.

Thomas "Stonewall" Jackson (1824–1863), a leading Confederate general in the Civil War, was born in Clarksburg. He earned his nickname at the First Battle of Bull Run, in 1861, when his troops stood "like a stone wall" against the Union army. His soldiers defeated Union forces in 1862 in the Shenandoah Valley. He then joined Robert E. Lee's campaign to drive Union troops from Richmond. He also took park in the Southern victories at Antietam and Fredericksburg. He was wounded at the battle of Chancellorsville in 1863 by his own troops, who had mistaken him for an enemy. He died from his wounds.

Thomas "Stonewall" Jackson

Anna M. Jarvis (1864–1948), the founder of Mother's Day, was born near Grafton. After the death of her mother, in 1907, she began campaigning to have a day set aside for honoring mothers. The first Mother's Day was celebrated in Grafton on May 12, 1908. In 1914 President Woodrow Wilson proclaimed the second Sunday of each May as Mother's Day.

Don Knotts (1924–2006), a television and movie actor, was born in Morgantown, the son of farmers. He attended West Virginia University. Knotts is best known for his role on the *Andy Griffith Show* as Deputy Barney Fife.

John Knowles (1926–2001), born in Fairmont, is the author of the novel *A Separate Peace*, which tells the story of two friends attending a New England prep school during World War II.

Kathy Mattea (1959–), born in South Charleston, is a successful country singer. In 1990 she won a Grammy Award for Best Country Performer. Twice she has been named Female Vocalist of the Year by the Country Music Association.

George Armitage Miller (1920–) is a psychologist whose studies of language were pioneering works in psycholinguistics. From 1960 to 1967 he was the director of Harvard University's Center for Cognitive Studies. He is the author of many works on psychology, including *Language and Speech*. From 1989 to 1994 Miller served as program director of the McDonnell-Pew Program in Cognitive Neuroscience, during which time he created WordNet, a database used by linguists. He was born in Charleston.

Don Knotts

Francis H. Pierpont
(1814–1899), born near Morgantown, is known as the father of West Virginia. When Virginia seceded from the Union, Pierpont organized people loyal to the North in the western part of the state. At the Wheeling Convention he was named governor of the Restored State of Virginia, the seceding western Virginia area.

Francis H. Pierpont

Mary Lou Retton (1968–   ), the 1984 Olympic gold medal-winning gymnast, was born in Fairmont. She began gymnastics lessons at age seven and moved to Houston, Texas at age fourteen to train with Romanian coach Bela Karolyi. At age sixteen she became the first American ever to win an individual all-around gold medal in gymnastics. She also won two silver medals (vault and team competition) and two bronze medals (floor exercise and parallel bars). Her exuberant smile and spirit made her a popular athlete and put her on the front of the Wheaties cereal box. In 1997 Retton was inducted into the International Gymnastics Hall of Fame.

Walter Reuther (1907–1970), born in Wheeling, was the president of the United Automobile Workers union from 1946 until his death. He was also the president of the Congress of Industrial

Mary Lou Retton

Organizations (CIO) from 1952 to 1955. He engineered the merger of the American Federation of Labor (AFL) and the CIO in 1955 and served as vice president of the AFL-CIO between 1955 and 1968. Reuther had started working in a factory at age sixteen and soon became involved in union causes. During his career Reuther won annual wage increases based on productivity, cost-of-living raises, and health and pension benefits for union members.

James Rumsey (1743–1792) is often called the inventor of the steamboat. He demonstrated a steamboat on the Potomac River at Shepherdstown in 1787. Rumsey died before his second demonstration model was finished.

Soupy Sales (Milton Supman) (1926–   ), a radio and television comedian, grew up in Huntington with the name Milton Hines. He is called the world's leading authority on pie throwing, a trademark of his comedy act. Sales hosted his own TV show from 1953 to 1960. In 2005 Sales received his star on the Hollywood Walk of Fame.

Harry Ford Sinclair (1876–1956), born in Wheeling, founded Sinclair Oil, which later became Atlantic Richfield, one of the world's largest oil companies. Sinclair gained notoriety during the 1920s, when he was charged with bribery and conspiracy to defraud the government during the so-called Teapot Dome oil field scandal that rocked the Warren G. Harding presidency. He was acquitted.

Cyrus Vance (1917–2002) was the U.S. secretary of state from 1977 to 1980, while Jimmy Carter was president. He also served as secretary of the army, deputy secretary of defense, and as a U.S. delegate during the Paris peace conference on Vietnam. As secretary of state he was involved in the Strategic Arms Limitation Talks, the negotiations leading to the Israeli-Egyptian peace treaty of 1979, and the efforts to secure the release of U.S. hostages in Iran. Vance was born in Clarksburg.

Cyrus Vance

Booker T. Washington (1856–1915) was a highly respected educator and a black leader. The son of slaves, Washington was born in Franklin County, Virginia, and moved to Malden, West Virginia, with his family after the Civil War. In 1881 he became the first president of the Tuskegee Institute, an Alabama trade school for blacks. Under his leadership, the school became a major agricultural and industrial college for African Americans. Washington believed that blacks needed an education if they were to win equality and integration. He became a well-known public speaker and advised presidents Theodore Roosevelt and William Howard Taft on racial matters. *Up from Slavery* is Washington's well-known autobiography.

Jerome Alan "Jerry" West (1938–   ), born in Cheylan, is considered one of the greatest basketball players ever. In fourteen years with the Los Angeles Lakers he played on thirteen consecutive all-star teams. In the 1969–1970 season he led the National Basketball Association in scoring, with a 31.2-point average. Two years later he led the league in assists, with 747. When he retired in 1974, he ranked third in regular-season career scoring, with 25,192 points and had a career average of 27 points per game. West was inducted into the Basketball Hall of Fame in 1980. He later served as the coach and general manager of the Lakers. In 2005 West Virginia University retired West's jersey number 44, the first number so honored by the school. West's son, Jonnie, played for West Virginia University in 2006.

Chuck Yeager (1923–   ) was the first person to travel faster than the speed of sound. Born in Myra, he enlisted in the army in 1941 and became an air force pilot in 1943. During World War II he flew sixty-four missions and shot down thirteen German aircraft. After the war he became a test pilot, and in 1947 he broke the sound barrier of 662 mph. In 1953 Yeager set a speed record of 1,650 mph. He wrote two books, *Yeager* and *Press On*.

Chuck Yeager

Beckley Exhibition Coal Mine (Beckley) Real coal miners guide visitors in remodeled mine cars through 1,500 feet of underground passageways in this former coal mine. A coal company house depicts the difficult life of a coal miner's family. You can also visit the mine museum and stay overnight in the campgrounds nearby.

Theatre West Virginia (Beckley) At the Cliffside Amphitheater in Grandview State Park, this theater company presents two musicals: *The Hatfields* and *McCoys* about the Hatfield-McCoy feud and *Honey in the Rock*, about the formation of the state.

Youth Museum of Southern West Virginia (Beckley) Experience the state's history at the heritage center, which features a mountain homestead, a one-room schoolhouse, a blacksmith shop, a loom room, and a frontier garden. You can also learn about the night skies at the planetarium and get a glimpse of 1880s railroad life through a collection of wood carvings.

State Capitol Complex (Charleston) The outstanding feature of the capitol is its gold-leaf rotunda, which is 5 feet higher than that of the U.S. capitol's dome. From the center of the 292-foot-high gold dome hangs a rock crystal chandelier weighing 2 tons. Also in the complex are the governor's mansion, the Booker T. Washington Memorial, and the State Museum, which traces state history, from Native American migration to the early twentieth century. Highlights include a settler's cabin, a general store, and Civil War exhibits.

State capitol

Criel Mound (South Charleston) This Adena mound was built as a burial site for chieftains during the first century C.E. It is the second-largest mound in the state, measuring 175 feet in diameter and 35 feet high.

Museum of Radio and Technology (Huntington) At this museum you can listen to recordings of old radio shows, tour exhibits on the history of radio, and trace the development of broadcasting, from radio to television to video.

West Virginia State Farm Museum (Point Pleasant) This 50-acre museum features thirty-one reconstructed buildings, including log cabins built in the early 1800s, a replica of an old Lutheran church, a one-room schoolhouse, a print shop, a doctor's office, a country store, a blacksmith shop, an herb garden, railroad cars, and farm equipment.

Grave Creek Mound State Park (Moundsville) This is the largest conical prehistoric burial mound of its kind. It measure 69 feet high and 295 feet in diameter. The Grave Creek Mound was built more than two thousand years ago by the Adena people. The nearby Delf Norona Museum and Cultural Center displays Native American artifacts from 1000 B.C.E. to 1 C.E.

The Palace of Gold (Moundsville) This palace was dubbed America's Taj Mahal by the *New York Times* because of its elaborate rooms, which are decorated with more than forty varieties of imported marble and onyx. The grounds also include the Imperial Elephant Restaurant and the Court of Roses gardens.

Oglebay Park (Wheeling) This park contains gardens, greenhouses, and a glass museum. A computerized light-and-sound show on Schenk Lake dazzles visitors. An 1863 train tours the Good Children's Zoo, where you can see more than two hundred North American animal species.

Independence Hall (Wheeling) If you're a Civil War buff, you'll want to visit the former capitol of the Restored Government of Virginia, now a museum and part of the Civil War Discovery Trail. Independence Hall once served as a customhouse, a post office, and a federal court, and was the site of the Second Wheeling Convention, where the state's Declaration of Independence was written.

West Virginia Penitentiary (Wheeling) Walk through the first territorial prison in the state and experience the dreary Alamo Cell Block, where the worst of the inmates spent twenty-two hours a day. Murals painted by inmates decorate the walls.

Pricketts Fort State Park (Fairmont) At this park you can learn about eighteenth-century life in West Virginia from costumed guides and craftspeople. The reconstructed fort is similar to one built on the same site in 1774. The amphitheater features presentations about the pioneers who settled the area.

Jackson's Mill Historic Area (Weston) This museum is located on the original 5-acre site of Stonewall Jackson's boyhood home. An old mill, blacksmithing equipment, carpentry tools, and weaving equipment are on display. Two furnished eighteenth-century log cabins are also on the grounds.

Berkeley Castle (Berkeley Springs) This half-scale copy of Sir William Berkeley's castle in England was built in 1885. (Berkeley was the third colonial governor of Virginia.) Called by some a Victorian folly, the castle features a large, stone-walled ballroom, a wide, curved staircase, a tower room, and an antiques collection.

James Rumsey Historical Monument and Museum (Shepherdstown) A park and monument mark the site on the Potomac River where James Rumsey launched the first steamboat in 1787. The museum houses a half-size working replica of that boat.

Hays-Gerrard House (Gerrardstown) Built in 1743, this is one of the oldest known buildings in West Virginia. A ladder and trapdoor provide access to the second floor of this two-story stone house.

Harpers Ferry National Historical Park (Harpers Ferry) The highlights of this 2,300-acre park are the six Paths Through History: Industry, John Brown, Civil War, African-American History, Environmental History, and Transportation. Other attractions include the Industry Museum, the Wetlands exhibit, John Brown's Fort, the Black Voices Museum, the Civil War Museum, and Jefferson Rock.

Harpers Ferry National Historical Park

Blackwater Falls State Park (Davis) You can enjoy hiking, riding, picnicking, nature programs, and other outdoor activities at this lovely park, but most people come to view the 65-foot-high Blackwater Falls.

Smoke Hole Caverns (Petersburg) This underground world contains one of the world's longest ribbon stalactites, a lake, and a stream. The caverns were used by Native Americans to smoke meat and by settlers to make moonshine. They were also used to store ammunition during the Civil War.

Cass Scenic Railroad (Cass) Take a ride on an old steam locomotive past mountain views to the top of Bald Knob, the second-highest peak in the state. You will pass through Cass, which was a large lumber community at the beginning of the twentieth century and is now one of the best preserved lumber company towns in the country.

Lost World Caverns (Lewisburg) Here you can explore large rooms below the surface and marvel at the stalagmite, stalactite, and flowstone formations. One formation is more than 40 feet high and 25 feet around. The main cavern at Lost World is 1,000 feet long and nearly 75 feet wide.

North House Museum (Lewisburg) This restored home from 1820 is noted for its fine architectural detail, such as elaborate, hand-carved woodwork. Now a museum, it displays military and civilian items from the Revolutionary and Civil War periods, including a covered wagon.

President's Cottage (White Sulphur Springs) This was the first private cottage built at the Greenbrier Hotel, a historic spa founded at the sulphur springs discovered by settlers in 1778. This cottage was named President's Cottage because five pre-Civil War presidents vacationed at the spa. In 1932 the cottage became a museum with exhibits detailing the Greenbrier's colorful history.

Cass Scenic Railroad

Can you name West Virginia's oldest town? Both Shepherdstown and Romney claim the honor. Shepherdstown was originally established by Thomas Shepherd, who laid out 50 acres of his land into lots and streets. He then asked the Virginia House of Burgesses for a bill of incorporation. He filed his bill six days before a similar bill was filed for Romney. Both bills were signed on the same day in 1762, but Romney's bill was signed first. So technically, Romney is the oldest town.

It took twenty-four years to complete the B&O Railroad between Baltimore, Maryland, and the Ohio River. Two crews, one working west from Baltimore and one working east from Wheeling, met in the Grave Creek Valley, 18 miles east of Wheeling, on Christmas Eve, 1852. At the time the B&O was the longest railroad in the world, and it was probably the most difficult to build—it had to pass through the rugged Allegheny Mountains.

Find Out More

If you want to find out more about West Virginia, look in your local library or bookstore for the following titles:

GENERAL STATE BOOKS

Mozier, Jeanne. *Way Out in West Virginia: A Must Have Guide to the Oddities and Wonders of the Mountain State.* Charleston, WV: Quarrier Press, 2004.

Smolan, Rick. *West Virginia: 24/7.* London: DK Adult, 2004.

Williams, John Alexander. *West Virginia: A History.* Morgantown: West Virginia University Press, 2001.

SPECIAL INTEREST BOOKS

Castro, James E. *South West Virginia: Coal Country.* Mt. Pleasant, SC: Arcadia Publishing, 2004.

Hudnall, William Roosevelt. *Kelly's Creek Chronicles: The Illustrated Diary of James Alexander Jones, a West Virginia Coalminer, 1870–1939.* New Canton, VA: Kelly's Creek Publishers, 2005.

Wallbridge, Charlie and Ward Eister. *A Canoeing & Kayaking Guide to West Virginia.* Birmingham, AL: Menasha Ridge Press, 2003.

West Virginia Government

www.legis.state.wv.us/Educational/Kids_Page/kids.html
Here's a Web site written specifically for kids. Learn about the state government and play games.

West Virginia

www.state.wv.us
You can find all kinds of information about West Virginia on this Web site.

Blue Ridge Country

www.blueridgecountry.com/hatmac/hatmac.html
If you want to learn all about the Hatfields and the McCoys, this is the place to do it.

The Story of West Virginia

www.americaslibrary.gov/cgi-bin/page.cgi/es/wv
The Library of Congress has gathered interesting facts about West Virginia history at this Web site.

Index

Page numbers in **boldface** are illustrations and charts.

Nancy Hoffman is a part-time newspaper writer and a full-time mother. She lives in Nashville, Tennessee with her husband, Tony, and their daughters, Eva and Chloe. Hoffman worked in public television, including three years as a producer for West Virginia Public Television.

Joyce Hart used to live in the nation's capital, and on weekends she would travel to West Virginia. The mountains roads, the lush forests, and the rushing rivers replenished her energy. Now Hart lives in a setting somewhat similar to West Virginia. After a short walk from her home, she can overlook the Puget Sound or the Hood Canal in another mountain state, the state of Washington.